STARTUP 101

The Entrepreneurs Tangible
Resources for Success

FREDRICK HINER

Copyright © 2016 by Fredrick Hiner
BDC Publishing

STARTUP 101
ISBN:1539035360 ISBN-13: 978-1539035367

Book interior design: FH
Cover design: FH

All rights reserved. No portion of this book may be reproduced or transmitted, in any form, or by any means, electronic or mechanical, including photocopying, recording, or using any storage and retrieval system, known now or developed in the future, without written permission from the author or the publisher, except in the case of brief quotations embodied in critical articles and/or reviews.

Printed in the United States of America

DEDICATION

This book is dedicated to all you Entrepreneurs about to embark on the wildest, hardest, crazy and to some very rewarding journey of business. ONLY those who are really serious about success will grasp the resources in this book and fully grip its reality.

CONTENTS

Introduction	5
1 FIRST THINGS FIRST MONEY	8
2 TAXES AND CREDITS	23
3 PEO'S	37
4 ANGEL INVESTORS	47
5 VENTURE CAPITAL	58
6 ECONOMIC INCENTIVES	71
7 MICRO ENTERPISES	82
8 HOW TO GET A LOAN	94
9 SBA	105
10 EQUIPMENT LEASING	113
11 FINANCIAL INCLUSION	134

INTRODUCTION E

ENTREPRENUERS

In this book, each chapter explains the financial resources that are essential to the life and viability of your Startup Business. I designed this book for you so that it can introduce, teach, and provide insight to the resources you need right now.

Most entrepreneurs start a company because of the hopes and passions that drive them. But, my question for you is, "do you feel that you have the support and are fully equipped to start a business?" What does that really mean? Statistics show that most people start a business to build a legacy for their family. I started my business for that reason, but it was just a small idea that grew exponentially in a matter of months; it was a two hundred-million-dollar vehicle to success within a year and later I lost it all in a day.

Can you imagine all the preparation it took to start that large of a business and to hire all the right professionals who had my back? It is a complicated process, and if you're not careful, the unknowns will creep up on you and destroy you in seconds.

How is that for hope, passion, feeling supported and equipped! I was devastated, my wife and family were shocked. The entire company felt like we had an avalanche in the middle of the desert. I lost everything I owned and almost lost my wife and kids, which is why I am writing this book just for you. My hope is to save families from all the unknown dangers of business by providing simple resources that could save your family, business, and legacy.

These resources are also a secret to a failure prevention model. What I mean is, you want to avoid building with the same business model that 93% of all startup companies that fail in the US actually use, which is called the OWNER OPERATED BUSINESS MODEL.

The resources in this book use the principle of absentee business model concepts. You see, the owner operated business model requires you to build the company to depend on you, when the absentee business model requires you to build your company to depend on a system. This allows more time with your family. In this country 60% of the divorces can attribute their failure to the 93% startup business failures in this country. You need to understand and capitalize on these resources if you want to experience your purpose and goals for starting the business!

FIRST THINGS FIRST—MONEY

You need Money

NOW, I WOULD LIKE to talk about money. Money is an important factor in life; just ask your spouse if you have one. It seems to have the same twisty vows as a marriage; it can make you better or worse. Money can be your worst enemy or your best friend, it just depends on whether you need it or not (no pun intended).

Many entrepreneurs and their families are in a world of hurt. Not because they are bad people but because when they started their business they started with the resources they thought was available. Let us consider a typical scenario a male contractor is in and it would look something like this: the wife feels second to the first wife (their job); their heart cries out for more time with the wife and kids, but they can't make it tonight; and the projects don't have enough money to complete themselves.

The pressure is building, the bills are slipping, the wife is cracking, the children are needy, and they are trying to dig themselves out of the hole and get ahead at the same time, but the problem is, they need more help—keep reading.

A money solution seems to be the only way to recovery! In that case, you better know something about money. As a business owner, if I said you could qualify for the cash this week to complete every project, purchase order and or contract you have up-front, would that interest you? Of course it would, so let us first learn the principles of financing using "Factoring".

To do business right you must have three things: the right education, the right team, and the right amount of money. The right education means more

than a trade skill; it also means some business skills that apply to the industry you are working in. The right team means people who can
take you where you want to go and tell you if you can't get there the way you're heading. The right amount of money— well, that is the most common mistake made by startup business owners, not starting with or asking for the right amount of money.

Let us look at the tools, vehicles, and mechanisms that work to build a successful startup business, especially in today's ecosystem of leveraging. Many businesses suffer to larger corporations because they don't leverage their assets in order to remain competitive and progressive, while attempting to increase sales. The major issue is having enough cash on hand to maintain an operating budget, while trying to develop and expand the company's distribution or services.

This is where leveraging your assets comes into play. For example, will you have clients that take 30, 50 or 60 days to pay their invoices? Although having slow paying clients is expected in today's business environment, they make managing cash flow a very difficult task. Paying suppliers, salaries and rent becomes a challenge because the cash flow is unpredictable. However, there is a way to solve this problem and make every project, purchase order and contract have predictable funding. The solution involves factoring your invoices.

What is Factoring?

Factoring is a financing tool that allows you to grow and expand by leveraging the weight of your business without credit and co-signers. For instance, through factoring you can get your invoices paid in as little as two days. Factoring provides your company with the necessary capital to operate the business, pay suppliers and grow. However, factoring is not a business loan. Rather, factoring involves selling your invoices at a discount for immediate cash. The factoring company waits to be paid by your client or customer, while you get immediate use of the funds.

Factoring is a financial transaction whereby a business sells its accounts receivable (i.e., invoices) to a third party (called a factor) at a discount.3 Invoice factoring can easily be integrated to any business and works as follows:

- You deliver goods or services and invoice for them.
- You sell the invoice to the factor. They give you the

- first installment of 70% to 90% of your invoice. This is called the advance.
- You get immediate funds to run your business
- Once your client pays the factoring company, you
- get the second installment (of 10% to 30%) and you are charged a small fee for the transaction. This is called the rebate.

One major advantage of factoring is that it is easier to obtain than a business loan. Furthermore, the factoring company can set the financing line in about a week. The biggest requirement for approval is that you do business with credit worthy clients.

Although you do not have to borrow against your outstanding accounts receivable invoices, your business maintains an active business line of credit for whenever you need it.

So why would anyone want to use factoring? Because it will allow you to grow your business and allow you to accept contracts that you normally couldn't fund because you don't have the cash reserves to make payroll or purchase inventory or supplies.

Who is Factoring?

Businesses of all sizes that make or distribute products and/or provide services to other businesses in virtually every industry can employ receivables factoring services. The main requirement is to simply have commercial accounts receivable, payable from other businesses or government entities.[1]

Accounts receivable factoring creates a line of credit which contains available funds that you can factor against in order to receive a cash advance on assets you already own. This form of business financing does not require strong business financials, positive cash flow, and established business credit. In addition, the factoring company provides the collection service, who works with the client's customer directly. It secures its position by basing its funding decision on the customer's credit, rather than that of the client, and then applying a lien on the accounts receivables.[2]

In the mad rush in the factoring industry, many distinctions were lost. Some truth, however, could not be escaped: factoring companies offer

---

[1] www.firstcapital.com/invoice_factoring.html

[2] www.rivierafinance.com/accounts-receivable-line-of-credit.asp

funding without debt. A bank loan, by definition, is debt.[3]

Here is a simple example: you have $10,000 in accounts receivable that will be paid in less than 30 days, but you need capital today to meet various business obligations. The factoring company purchases the invoice from you and provides cash equal to 80% of the accounts receivable, or $8,000 immediately. A 20% reserve, or $2,000, is held until the factored receivables are paid in full by your customer or client. Assuming that a 3% discount rate applies and all of the factored invoices are paid within 30 days, you are paid your remaining $1,700 when your client pays the invoice. The total cost of factoring to the business is $300.

Why Use Factoring?

Because it will allow you to grow your business and allow you to accept contracts, purchase orders, and or invoiced projects that you normally couldn't fund because you don't have the cash reserves to make payroll or purchase inventory or supplies.

To summarize the benefits of Factoring:

- Factoring is not a loan and does not show up as a debt owned by your company.
- Factoring is much faster to fund than loans.
- Invoices can be paid daily or weekly as needed.
- It is usually not dependent on the credit rating of your company.
- It is usually not dependent of the assets of your company.
- It is not dependent on the number of years you have been in business.
- Your balance sheet is strengthened because you have more cash on hand.
- You are not required to factor all your receivables.
- You can create a source of unlimited capital.
- You become more "bankable," allowing you to get that bank line of credit.
- You get professional credit checking and monitoring of your new and existing customers at no charge to you.

Why is Factoring Unique?

The construction industry is unique when it comes to factoring because

---

[3] www.interstatecapital.com/factoring_articles/10-lesson-learned-borrow-against-fixed-assets-factor-your-account

of retainage. Retainage, as used in the construction industry, is an amount of money, usually 10% that is withheld by the general contractor until the entire project is completed by the sub-contractor. So, if you are the subcontractor that installs the foundation for a new building, even though your work is complete, you may not receive the last 10% of your payments until the building is entirely complete, which can be anywhere from 30 days to one year later. As you will see in the following example and case study, retainage is not considered when an invoice is factored.

Let's assume you have $100,000 in accounts receivable that will be paid in less than 30 days, but you need capital today to meet various business obligations. We are also assuming that there is a 10% retainage. The factor purchases the invoices from you and provides cash equal to 75% of the accounts receivable less retainage, or $67,500 immediately ($90,000*.75). The factor maintains a 25% reserve, or $22,500, until the factored receivables are paid. (Note that the last 10% is the retainage that is not included as part of the factoring transaction.) Assuming that a 3.5% discount rate applies and all of the factored invoices are paid within 30 days, you are paid your remaining $19,000 when the invoice is paid by your client. The total cost of factoring to the business is $3500.

The Cost of Factoring: Case Study[4]

Drywall Contractor (as a Subcontractor) on a large VA facility.

- **Approved Line of Credit:** $400,000
- **Advance Rate:** 75%
- **Advance Discount Rate:** 2.25% for the first 30 days
- **Factoring Fee:** 2.25% for all outstanding invoices after 30 days
- **Funds Control Fee:** 1% of the contract amount payable at the time of processing each invoice that was factored
- **Project Cost:** $1 million
- **Retainage:** 10%
- **Project Duration:**
- **12 months Average Invoice:** The first invoice was $350,000 and covered a substantial amount of material costs. The next three invoices averaged $100,000 and covered mostly payroll, but also additional material.

By the fifth month, the contractor was operating with positive cash flow

---

[4] CFMA BP, Jan- Feb 2011, "The Cost of Money: Factoring Working Capital," Earl Harper, p 5.

and did not need to factor any additional receivables. However, the contractor kept the funds control program in place for the duration of the project in case she needed to factor additional receivables toward the end of the project.

Average Aging of Invoices: 30 days

Advances and Fees for the Four Invoices Factored:
- Invoice #1 - Advance was $236,250 and fee was $7,088
- Invoices #2-4 - Advances totaled $67,500 and fees were $2,025 each
- Funds control fee was 1% of the face amount for each invoice, net of retainage (total of $5,850)

Total Real Costs for Factoring the Project:
- Advance Discount Fee: $13,163 to borrow $438,750
- Funds Control Fee: $10,000 (since the contractor used funds control on the entire project)

Total Cost:
- $23,163 (approximately 2.3% of the total project)

Note: The ability to pay entrepreneurs and suppliers in net 30-45 days or less allowed this contractor to reduce those expenses by more than 10%, turning the factoring into a profitable subcontractor.

In addition, since she used funds control on the entire project, she was able to negotiate additional credit for both entrepreneurs and suppliers in the later stages of the project.

Frequently Asked Questions

1. *How soon can a factoring proposal be issued?*
    a. A proposal can be issued usually within two to three days after the proper information is submitted.
2. *Is accounts receivable funding a new financing option?*
    a. No, accounts receivable funding is one of the oldest forms of financing. It has been around in one form or another for more than 40 years.
    b. Until the mid-1980s, most people thought accounts receivable funding was only used in the textile and garment industries.
    c. Today, accounts receivable funding is a widely used and

viable financing solution for all types of businesses that extend credit terms to their customers.

3. *How can accounts receivable funding help my business?*
   a. By providing an immediate source of cash flow for your company. You can use this cash to provide working capital, meet payroll, pay taxes, replenish inventory, increase advertising, purchase equipment, improve your credit rating, and more.

4. *How is accounts receivable funding from a factor different from a line of credit from a bank?*
   a. When making a funding decision, a factor focuses on the creditworthiness of your customers, while banks will focus on your company's financial history and cash flow. In addition, since accounts receivable funding is not a loan, there is no debt on your company's balance sheet. Best of all, the factor will make a quick funding decision, while banks may take weeks—even months—to approve a loan.

5. *Will my company be eligible for accounts receivable funding if it has a bank loan or a line of credit?*
   a. If a bank has a lien on your company's accounts receivable, you will not be able to also factor your receivables.
   b. Most factors will work with the bank to subordinate that lien in their favor. Because this is a common occurrence, some banks will accommodate the request, depending on the assets of the business.

6. *My company owes back taxes. Can I still apply for accounts receivable funding?*
   a. Yes, tax problems are handled on a case-by-case basis. Please let the factor know immediately so that they can dis- cuss the payoff of your back taxes or a lien subordination with the IRS.

7. *I have had a past bankruptcy. Is accounts receivable funding still an option?*
   a. Yes, most factors will still consider your application even if you have credit problems or a past bankruptcy.

8. *What information does a factor need from my company to begin the accounts receivable funding process?*
   a. Each factor has their own application that needs to be completed. Additionally, they may request your current accounts receivable list and a list of your clients (so they can evaluate their creditworthiness).
   b. If you are in the service, distribution or even construction industries, they will request information on your business to ensure your ability to deliver on the contract.

9. *Which customers would be good candidates for accounts receivable funding?*
    a. Ideally, the factor would like to fund all of your customers. Unfortunately, not all companies have a strong enough credit rating or a history of paying their suppliers. Because of this, a good majority of factors will provide some form of credit checking to ensure the viability of your client to meet their obligations.
10. *Can the factoring company purchase only a portion of my company's invoices?*
    a. Absolutely, but remember that your fee is typically based on the dollar volume of the receivables.
    b. So a higher dollar volume of receivables sold on a regular basis can result in more competitive rates.
11. *What is the Advanced Rate?*
    a. (As high as 95%) The Advanced Rate is the percentage advanced on your invoices. For example, you sent a $10,000 invoice to be factored, the factor advances 90% of that invoice to you ($9,000) via wire transfer to your bank account within 24 hours.
    b. The additional 10% of the invoice is sent to you by the factor (less service fee) once the invoice is paid by your customer.
    c. Typical advances are 75% to 90% of the invoice, but the actual Advanced Rate (as high as 95%) is based on the age of the invoice (10, 30, 60, 90, 120 days), and the financial strength and credit worthiness of your customers.

Factoring can save your business. I have seen the simple principle of factoring, provide the longevity a company needed to sustain them in the 5-year climb. Your situation might be unique, but think outside the box; it could save the day.

2

TAX AND CREDITS

A Government Incentive

THE FEDERAL GOVERNMENT is spending around $30,000 per year per person to keep people on public assistance; this is why they are more than happy to give you an income tax credit if you hire one or more of those people. In this chapter, I want to show you how to help reduce your annual startup cost and minimize our government debt which will add additional dollars to your bottom line by using various forms of tax credits.

Businesses across the U.S., in every state, have been doing it for years. Why not you? Again, the goal is to present you with the building blocks to start right and secure your marriage, family life and business, with actionable information that could bring stability and sustainability to your startup business as well as your home. One of the ways you can do that is with tax credits and tax incentives. Let me explain.

Let's assume that you will own a town and will hire 100 people who qualify for the tax credits. This could include one person at the bank, two people at the hardware store, four part-time farm hands and ten folks at the manufacturing plant. Each business may not think it is important to be a part of this program, but if all 100 new hires earned the $2,400 maximum credit allowance from our government, the community as a whole would see a $240,000 increase in bottom line revenue. What could your Startup business do with an extra $2,400.00 per employee?

What are Employer Tax Credits?

A tax credit is a sum deducted from the total amount a taxpayer owes to the state or federal government. A tax credit may be granted for various types of taxes, such as an income tax, property tax, or value added tax (VAT). From a buyer, a tax on the purchase price; from a seller, tax on a product, material or service; and from an accounting— distribution. Tax credits may be granted in recognition of taxes already paid, as a subsidy, or to encourage investment or other behaviors.

On December 18, 2015, President Obama signed into law the Protecting Americans from Tax Hikes Act of 2015 (the PATH Act) that extends and modifies the WOTC Program (Work Opportunity Tax Credit) and the Empowerment Zones. In summary, the PATH Act:

- ✓ Retroactively reauthorizes the WOTC program target groups for a five-year period, from December 31, 2014 to December 31, 2019.
- ✓ Extends the Empowerment Zones for a two-year period, from December 31, 2014 to December 31, 2016.
- ✓ Introduces a new target group, Qualified Long-term Unemployment Recipients, for new hires that begin to work for an employer on or after January 1, 2016 through December 31, 2019.

START UP 101

Below is a chart that highlights the major programs offered by the Federal Government.

In some systems, tax credits are "refundable" to the extent that they exceed the relevant tax. Tax systems may grant tax credits to businesses or individuals, and such grants vary by type of credit.

Employer tax credits are credits that the Federal and State Governments give to companies like your startup that will hire and retain certain disadvantaged individuals. These individuals are typically individuals on public assistance. The programs, at the Federal level are the Work Opportunity Tax Credit Program (**WOTC**), the Welfare to Work Program (**W2W**) and the Empowerment Zone (**EZ**)/Enterprise Community (**EC**)/Renewal Community Programs (**RC**).

Each program has its own qualifications and its own calculations on how to receive the various tax credits. Each year there are adjustments to the

Federal Programs	How is it calculated?	What is the maximum?	What are the criteria?	Who funds the program?
Welfare to work Tax Credits	Year 1: 40% of $10,000 earnings. Year 2: 50% of $10,000 earnings.	Year 1 $4,000 Year 2 $5,000	Long-term welfare recipient. Must work 400 hours each year	Federal Government
Empowerment Zones, Enterprise Communities, Renewal Communities Tax Credits	20% of the 1st $15,000 in earnings for EZ, EC and 10% of the first $15,000 for RC.	$3,000 or $1,500	Must live and work in the EZ, EC, or RC	Federal Government
HIRE Act Credits	Employer does not pay employer portion of FICA	FICA maximum times 6.2%	Employee must have started work between 2-3-10 and not 12-31-10 and not more than 40 hours in the 60 days prior to starting with the company	State
Each state has programs that reduce a company's state, city, or local taxes	Depends on the state	Depends on the state	Depends on the state	State

programs offered by the Federal Government, such as the HIRE Act, which was only offered in 2010.

There are so many ways for you to take advantage of this; I cannot possibly list them all. What I can tell you is that you would be surprised what credits and incentives you may qualify for. In this chapter, I want to answer common questions to explain what are the advantages and how can you capitalize on these tax credits and incentives to increase your startup business and secure your legacy.

Frequently Asked Questions:

1. *How Do Employees Qualify?* Follow this link and you may be able to integrate this into your three and five-year startup plan. https://www.doleta.gov/business/incentives/opptax/forms.cfm to fill out these forms. Many companies are surprised at how many employees qualify for one of many different tax programs. Some even qualify for multiple programs. This knowledge will enhance the predictable startup cost for you.
2. Why Does the Government Give Tax Credits? Largely, tax credits exist to reduce the welfare rolls and to get the disadvantaged into employee roles. It costs the government $25-$30,000 per year to keep someone on public assistance.
3. How Can I Qualify for Employer Tax Credits? Employers don't qualify. Employees do. All new hires are asked a series of questions and are asked to sign a form. This form, along with our research, determines if the employee is eligible for certification. Once certified, the employer earns tax credits. The longer the employee is employed, the higher the tax credit up to the allowable maximum.
4. How Do Tax Credits Affect my Bottom Line? Tax credits are a reduction in your federal tax liability and a dollar for dollar increase to your bottom line. If you are making a profit and paying federal and/or state income taxes, you can reduce your quarterly tax deposits by the amount of the credit. As an example, say your taxable income was $100,000. Assuming normal tax rates, you would pay $34,000 in taxes and keep $66,000. If you have $18,000 in credits, you would reduce the tax liability of $34,000 to $16,000, retaining $84,000, which is $18,000 more. As a public company, this goes right to shareholder value, increasing earnings per share and market value.

5. What Amount of Credit am I Likely to Get? On average, 10-12% of your new hires will qualify for a minimum of $1,500.00 each in credits9. If you grow to 600 employees and your turnover rate is 30% (including replacements and growth positions) then you will have, on average, 180 new hires. Of the 180, 10% of them, or 18 employees will be tax credit eligible.
6. Based on company averages as of 11/10/14. Actual numbers depend on many factors. Each eligible employee will average $1,500.00, so your tax credit for the first year will be $27,000.00. These credits continue as you continue to hire people. Some individuals will qualify under the Welfare to Work program, and if you keep them employed for two years, you can earn as much as $9,000 in credits. There are companies that work to improve the averages by identifying pre-certified employees for open positions and assisting companies in ways to retain those individuals. Employees have to work a minimum of 120 hours to be eligible for WOTC credits and W2W.
7. What are the Categories? There are eleven categories of employees that are eligible—those on food stamps, welfare, ex-felons, supplemental security income, state funded disability recipients, to name a few. President Obama added two new categories through the 2009 stimulus package: disconnected youth and unemployed veterans.
8. I'm an S-Corp (or partnership or LLC or LLP); are Tax Credits Available to Me? Yes, they simply pass to your individual return to reduce your individual federal tax burden. This also applies to LLCs and LLPs.
9. I'm Really Busy. How Will This Affect the Running of My Business? Each program can be customized to your needs. In most cases, it will not interrupt your daily workflow. The only "discomfort" is that all new hires have to sign three additional forms, and you will need to send those forms to a tax credit specialist that you choose to resource. This only takes a few minutes with each new applicant/new hire. Or, they can enroll online, which even takes less time.
10. How Much Will it Cost Me? There is no charge by most tax credit specialist unless they can identify and deliver bookable tax credits. Fees are billed on a quarterly or monthly basis as tax credits are identified and earned. The actual cost is dependent

upon the services need because every business is different, but it is a small percent of the money they save you.

11. What are My Obligations and/or Commitments? You will need to sign a very specific power of attorney so they can represent you as agent for two specific tax forms which they will file on your behalf. In addition, a general agreement needs to be signed which outlines the terms. This agreement is cancelable at any time.
12. What's the Catch? There is no catch. 15% of U.S. companies are saving significant taxes by processing their employees. These programs were created by Federal and State governments to help the "difficult to employ" find employment and get off the welfare rolls, thereby saving the government considerable amounts of money. This book provides an easy solution to companies that want to improve their profits by taking advantage of these little known opportunities.
13. Can My Accountant Do This? Most accountants will help with the year-end processing of your tax returns but are not set up to handle the research and filing requirements of this program. The outsourced tax specialist you hire will have created proprietary databases that allow them to find more qualified persons than a typical accountant.
14. What is the typical process and relationship with the tax credit specialist? Let's take the headache out of the process and generate income tax credits or refunds for your new startup. The fees are a percentage of what are delivered. There are never any startup fees, contract fees, or estimated fees. It's truly a win-win. Most agreements are cancelable at any time. It's the proverbial "free money" that every company is entitled to.

You will simply ask each new hire to fill out three additional forms at date of hire. It should take no more than 4-5 minutes per new hire. At the end of each quarter, the tax credit resource will provide the calculation of the amount of credits the company has earned. At the end of the year, all tax documents for the company are prepared and copies of all calculations and certifications are attached. They will guarantee accuracy of the calculations.

Many systems offer various incentives for businesses to make investments in property or operate in particular areas. Credits may be offered against income or property taxes and are generally nonrefundable to the extent they exceed taxes otherwise due. The credits may be offered to individuals as well as entities. The nature of the credits available varies highly by jurisdiction.

Many sub-Federal jurisdictions (states, counties, cities, etc.) within the U.S. offer income or property tax credits for particular activities or expenditures. Examples include credits similar to the Federal research and employment credits, property tax credits granted by cities (often called abatements) for building facilities within the city, etc. These items often are negotiated between a business and a governmental body and are specific to a particular business and property.

U.S. income tax has numerous nonrefundable business credits. In most cases, any amount of these credits in excess of current year tax may be carried forward to offset future taxes, with limitations. The credits include the following and are available to individuals and businesses:

- Alternative motor vehicle credit: several credits are available for purchase of varying types of non-gasoline powered vehicles,[5]
- Alternative fuel credits:
    o a credit based on the amount of production of certain non-petroleum fuels,[6]
    o Disaster relief credits,[7]
    o Credits for employing individuals in certain areas or those formerly on welfare or in targeted groups,
    o Credit for increasing research expenses;
    o And a variety of industry specific credits.

---

[5] See "Alternative Motor Vehicle tax Credit" at www.irs.gov.

[6] See "Fuel Tax Credits and Refunds" at www.irs.gov.

[7] See www.irs.gov/irs/article/0,,id=203056,00.html for the article called, "Tax law changes related to disaster relief."

3

PEO$

THIS MIGHT SEEM LIKE an odd chapter to include because it is not a direct funding resource, but I chose to include it because it saves the startup business owner time and also moves the liability for having employees to the Professional Employer Organization (PEO). I believe that every startup company should consider outsourcing to a PEO or staffing agency. It reduces HR liabilities and removes the weight of internal maintenance so you can have more time for family and corporate development. A part of my commitment to you will be connecting your startup with a few national providers of outsourcing services, which include Human Resources, Payroll Administration, Employee Benefits, Workers' Compensation and Risk Management.

These Professional Employer Organizations, or PEOs, are some of the largest and most respectable in the nation. As of 2014, there were more than 700 PEOs operating in the United States, covering 2-3 million workers.[8] PEOs operate in all fifty U.S. states. Their size, scope, financial stability and affiliation with major insurance carriers help give you the peace of mind in knowing that their service requirements are entrusted to companies that are truly the best in their class.

What is a PEO?

A professional employer organization (PEO) is a single source provider

---

[8] http://www.napeo.org/peoindustry/industryfacts.

of integrated services which enables Startup business owners to cost-effectively outsource the management of human resources, employee benefits, payroll and workers' compensation and other strategic services, such as recruiting, risk/safety management, and training and development. It does this by hiring a client company's employees, thus becoming their employer of record for tax purposes and insurance purposes. This practice is known as co-employment.

One of the items, which I believe needs to be changed in the small business industry, is the owner-operated business model. In the owner-operated model, the entrepreneur is responsible for everything associated with the business, i.e. sales, marketing, HR, payroll, etc. This concept might work for the small mom and pop store, but if an entrepreneur is serious about growing his or her business, they need to know what they do well. Items, which fall into the "I don't do well" category need to either be delegated to employees or outsourced. It is very important to listen to this statistic or you could lose your family, business and legacy.

The change in the age of the population between 1980 and today—the population of married men and women is considerably older now—the divorce rate has actually risen 40%. By these measures, after a brief pause in the recessionary year of 2009, the divorce rate peaked in 2011. "By 2010," they write, "almost half of every married American had divorced or separated by the time they reached their late 50's (http://family-studies.org/divorce-its-way-bigger-than-we-thought/)." What is even more shocking being that out of 2,118,000 marriages in the US, 60% of those are attributed to the 93% small business failure rates in the US. So my caution to you is to use every resource you can possibly find to provide time for your spouse and children.

The professional employer organization (PEO) is a resource that will return time and money to the startup business owner. It acts as the HR department for the startup business as it grows until it can justify hiring a full time HR specialist. It will do the routine tasks like payroll much more efficiently than the owner, who has to remember how to do it every two weeks. It stays current on tax law so the business does not receive any unexpected visits from the IRS. And it stays current on all other laws that could possibly affect a business, like the changes that came due to the passage of the new health care law.

PEO Business Model

In a co-employment contract, the PEO becomes the employer of record for tax purposes, filing paperwork under its own tax identification numbers.

The client company continues to direct the employees' day-to-day activities. PEOs charge a service fee for taking over the human resources and payroll functions of the client company; typically, this is from 3 to 15% of total payroll.14 This fee is in addition to the normal employee overhead costs, such as the employer's share of FICA, Medicare, and unemployment insurance withholding.

One key service usually provided by a PEO is to secure Workers Compensation insurance coverage for client companies. This is normally one of the key selling points stressed by a PEO—that a PEO can provide Workers Compensation insurance coverage at lower cost than client companies can obtain on an individual basis. While there is some merit to this assertion, it has also been an area of considerable controversy and litigation.

Essentially, a PEO obtains Workers Compensation coverage for its clients by negotiating insurance coverage that covers not just the PEO but also the client companies. This is allowed because legally the PEO is the co-employer of the workers at the client companies. There can be economies of scale that come into play, allowing a PEO to obtain Workers Compensation Insurance at a cost lower than the individual client companies can obtain on their own.

Effectively, PEO companies maintain a relationship with their clients on keeping updates of employee information. In light of this, Professional Employer Organizations successfully engage in improving practices of employment—this includes compliance, risk management and reducing liabilities. With the professionalism of PEOs, they provide management solutions that can benefit their clientele. Lastly, an important service is the presence of strategy and knowledge of the labor market. With this key aspect in mind, the PEO will opt to maximizing the competency in the labor market. PEOs can also offer basic levels of background and drug screening.

In the United States, many small to medium size professional services firms utilize PEOs to allow them to provide the kinds of benefit plans which otherwise could only be made available at a prohibitively high cost to both the employer and the employee.

Several variations on the PEO model exist, differing in the nature of the relationship formed between PEO and the client's company:

- Administrative Services Organizations (ASO) are similar to PEOs but do not create a co-employment relationship. Employees remain

- Pass-through agencies are staffing firms that act as the employer of record for independent entrepreneurs, but do not obtain work for them.
- Financial intermediaries, also called fiscal intermediaries, act as an employer of record for home healthcare workers who serve disabled persons.

So, how does the business model work? When you enter into a relationship with a Professional Employer Organization (PEO), a co-employment arrangement develops in which both the PEO and your startup have an employment relationship with the employee. The PEO contractually allocates and shares traditional employer responsibilities and liabilities with your startup company.

The list below illustrates the responsibilities, benefits and synergies between the PEO, your startup and your employees.

Client (you, the business owner):
- Hire/Release Employees with the PEO
- Supervise employees
- Manage and Operate Business
- Control Worksite Activities
- Focus on Business Development and Profitability
- Establish Worksite Policies and Procedures

Ensure Worksite Safety

Employee (the employees working for you, the business owner)
- Receive Comprehensive Benefits
- Receive On-Time and Accurate Payroll
- Are provided Professional Orientation and Employee Handbook
- Have a source to provide Assistance With Employment-Related Problems
- Should have Improved Employer-Employee Communication
- Will have Consistent Policies/Procedures
- Should have Enhanced Employee Morale

The PEO:
- Provides Professional Human Resources Services

- Provides and Administers Fortune 500 Company Benefit Packages
- Payroll Administration/Tax Guidance
- Workers' Compensation/Risk Management
- Cost Containment
- Legal and Regulatory Guidance and Compliance

How Does a PEO Benefit Your Company?

A partnership with a PEO means having access to a comprehensive suite of employment-related products and services. By outsourcing your day-to-day administrative tasks, you are able to focus your time and energy on what matters most to the success of your business: developing and retaining customers.

Here's what we can help you:

1. Payroll Administration. Through certified payroll experts who are dedicated to your account and can ensure that your employees are paid correctly and on time.
2. Employee Benefits. Through cost-effective, comprehensive Fortune 500-type benefits, we can transform your company into an employer of choice so you can attract and retain top professionals in your field of expertise.
3. Human Resources. Cost-effective solutions keep your company compliant with all federal and state employment laws and free from the burden of administrative tasks.
4. Risk Management. The outsourcing firm will carry full liability for your workers' compensation and help you to create and maintain a safe work environment in addition to providing expert underwriters, loss control specialists and claims managers.

When you partner with a PEO, you are able to take full advantage of its size, strength and relationship with leading benefits providers. By offering integrated, cost-effective solutions for your business, they provide remarkable value. Here is a testimony, one of the attendees at a trade show shared that he had created a relationship with a PEO about a year ago and it was the best thing he had ever done. He said that he has slept peacefully since then, knowing someone had his back covered. This man was able to focus on priorities rather than the maintenance of the company, and that enabled him to build his business and the economy. His family had the greatest benefit of all—more time with each other.

4

ANGEL INVESTORS

Does Everyone Have an Angel?

ANGEL INVESTORS ARE wealthy individuals who like to invest in small start-up enterprises. When they invest their money into a business, it is not considered a loan. Instead, they desire an agreeable percentage of stock or share in a company for their own financial gain.

This is something I enjoy—helping people succeed. In my consulting business, I learned to accept equity as a form of payment. As a farmer, we never were paid for the milk before it was produced. Likewise, this should be the way we do business, so I did not mind producing the fruit of my labors.

Most angels have experience in the industry of their investment and most likely are successful business owners themselves. They can act as effective, obliging advisors and mentors to entrepreneurs on how to make their business thrive. In addition, they can offer a large sum of money that may not be available from other sources. Angels often require a percentage of stock or shares in their invested companies. This means that entrepreneurs may have to give up some control of their businesses.

The term "angel" originally came from England and was borrowed by New York's Broadway enthusiasts where it was used to describe wealthy individuals who provided money for theatrical productions. I find this interesting because my true passion is to make and produce theatrical productions and films. And let me tell you from experience, it is difficult to fund a film or movie, and getting an investor for such a project is difficult, and for the investor, a high risk. As a partner with a film production company, and my active involvement in the movie industry, this term, "angel" really fits here.

In the Movies I liken this model to the movie, Angels in the Outfield. The original version was in 1951, starring Paul Douglas, Janet Leigh and Keenan Wynn. It's a story of a young woman reporter who blames the Pittsburgh Pirates' losing streak on the obscenely abusive manager. While she attempts to learn more about him for her column, he begins hearing the voice of an angel promising him help for the team if he will mend his ways. As he does so, an orphan girl, who is a Pirates fan and has been praying for the team, begins to notice angels on the ball field. Sure enough, the Pirates start winning, and McGovern tries to turn his life around. But can he keep his temper long enough for the Pirates to win the NL pennant?

That movie was before my time. The one I am familiar with is Walt Disney's 1994 rendition, starring Danny Glover, Tony Danza and Christopher Lloyd. The story is about a boy who has lost his mother and is living separated from his father. He prays for a chance to have a family if the California Angels win the pennant; angels are assigned to make that possible.

Where Do Angels Come From?

What is interesting about the plot in Angels in the Outfield is that not everyone can see them. The fact remains, it is not what they can see that matters most but how much of a difference it makes for success with angels in the outfield. The same is true for angel' investors. Angels come in two varieties: those you know and those you don't know. They may include professionals such as doctors and lawyers; business associates such as executives, suppliers and customers; and even other entrepreneurs. Unlike venture capitalists and bankers, many angels are not motivated solely by profit. Particularly if your angel is a current or former entrepreneur, he or she may be motivated as much by the enjoyment of helping a young startup business succeed as by the money he or she stands to gain. Angels are more likely than venture capitalists to be persuaded by an entrepreneur's drive to succeed, persistence and mental discipline. Angel investors vary widely, but they are typically willing to accept risk and demand little or no control in return for the chance to own a piece of a business that may be valuable someday.

Angel investing has soared in recent years as a growing number of individuals seek better returns on their money than they can get from traditional investment venues. Contrary to popular belief, most angels are not millionaires. Typically, they earn between $60,000 and $100,000 a year, which means there are likely to be plenty of them right in your own backyard.

In 1978, William Wetzel, then a professor at the University of New Hampshire and founder of its Center for Venture Research, completed a pioneering study on how entrepreneurs raised seed capital in the USA, and he began using the term "angel" regularly to describe the investors that supported these high-risk early-stage businesses.[9] Angels typically invest their own funds, unlike venture capitalists who manage the pooled money of others in a professionally managed fund.[10] Although typically reflecting the investment judgment of an individual, the actual entity that provides the funding may be a trust, business, limited liability company, investment fund, etc. A Harvard report by William R. Kerr, Josh Lerner, and Antoinette Schoar provides evidence that angel-funded startup companies are less likely to fail than companies that rely on other forms of initial financing.[11]

There is no "set amount" for angel investors, and the range can go anywhere from a few thousand to a few million dollars. Angel financing, while more readily available than venture financing, is still extremely difficult to raise.[12] However, some new models are developing that are trying to make this easier.[13] Many companies who receive angel funding are required to file a Form D with the Securities and Exchange Commission.

Angel investments bear extremely high risk and are usually subject to dilution from future investment rounds. As such, they require a very high return on investment. Angel investors are often retired entrepreneurs or executives who may be interested in angel investing for reasons that go beyond pure monetary return. These include wanting to keep abreast of current developments in a particular business arena, mentoring another generation of entrepreneurs, and making use of their experience and networks on a less than full-time basis. Thus, in addition to funds, angel

---

[9] http://definitions.uslegal.com/a/angel-funding/

[10] Joe Hadzima."All Financing Sources Are Not Equal". Boston Business Journal.

[11] http://hbswk.hbs.edu/item/6347.html?wknews=041910

[12] "Entrepreneur FAQ". California Investment Network. Retrieved 2011-09-27. "Angels are also extremely discerning in the projects that they will invest in (rejecting, on average, approximately 97% of the proposals submitted to them)."

[13] http://www.bbc.co.uk/news/10100885

investors can often provide valuable management advice and important contacts.

Classifications of Angels Allow me to be more specific concerning the types of ways to obtain angels investors. Angels can be classified into two groups: *affiliated* and *nonaffiliated.*

An *affiliated* angel is someone who has some sort of contact with you or your business but is not necessarily related to or acquainted[14] with you. A nonaffiliated angel has no connection with either you or your business.[15] It makes sense to start your investor search by seeking an affiliated angel since he or she is already familiar with you or your business and has a vested interest in the relationship. Let us look at possible Angels you may know.

Professionals. These include professional providers of services you now use—doctors, dentists, lawyers, accountants and so on. You know these people, so an appointment should be easy to arrange. Professionals usually have discretionary income available to invest in outside projects, and if they're not interested, they may be able to recommend a colleague who is.

Business associates.

These are people you come in contact with during the normal course of your business day. They can be divided into four subgroups:

> 1. Suppliers/vendors. The owners of companies who supply your inventory and other needs have a vital interest in your company's success and make excellent angels. A supplier's investment may not come in the form of cash but in the form of better payment terms or cheaper prices. Suppliers might even use their credit to help you get a loan.
> 2. Customers. These are especially good contacts if they use your product or service to make or sell their own goods. List all the customers with whom you have this sort of business relationship.
> 3. Employees. Some of your key employees might be sitting on unused equity in their homes that would make excellent collateral for a business loan to your business. There's no greater incentive to an employee than to share ownership in the company for which he or she works.

---

[14] http://www.entrepreneurship.org/en/resource-center/valuation-divergence.aspx

[15] http://www.entrepreneur.com/encyclopedia/term/82114.html

4. Competitors. These include owners of similar companies which you don't directly compete with. If a competitor is doing business in another part of the country and doesn't infringe on your territory, he or she may be an empathetic investor and may share, not only capital, but information as well.

The *nonaffiliated* angel category includes:

Professionals. This group can include lawyers, accountants, consultants and brokers whom you don't know personally or do business with. Middle managers. Angels in middle management positions start investing in small businesses for two major reasons. Either they're bored with their jobs and are looking for outside interests, or they're nearing retirement or fear they're being phased out.

Entrepreneurs. These angels are (or have been) successful in their own businesses and like investing in other entrepreneurial ventures. Entrepreneurs who are familiar with your industry make excellent investors. Approaching affiliated angels is simply a matter of calling to make an appointment.

To look for nonaffiliated angels, try these proven methods:

Advertising. The business opportunity section of your local newspaper or The Wall Street Journal is an excellent place to advertise for investors. Classified advertising is inexpensive, simple, quick and effective.

Business brokers. Business brokers know hundreds of people with money who are interested in buying businesses. Even though you don't want to sell your business, you might be willing to sell part of it. Since many brokers aren't open to the idea of their clients buying just part of a business, you might have to use some persuasion to get the broker to give you contact names. You'll find a list of local business brokers in the Yellow Pages under "Business Brokers."

Telemarketing. This approach has been called "dialing for dollars." First you get a list of wealthy individuals in your area. Then you begin calling them. Obviously, you have to be highly motivated to try this approach, and a good list is your most important tool. Look up mailing-list brokers in the Yellow Pages. If you don't feel comfortable making cold calls yourself, you can always hire someone to do it for you.

Networking. Attending local venture capital group meetings and other business associations to make contacts is a time-consuming approach but can be effective. Most newspapers contain an events calendar that lists when and where these types of meetings take place.

Intermediaries. These are firms that find angels for entrepreneurial companies. They're usually called "boutique investment bankers." This means they are small firms that focus primarily on small financing deals. These firms typically charge a percentage of the amount of money they raise for you. Ask your lawyer or accountant for the name of a reputable firm in your area.

Angel Funds. In most states you will find one or more organizations that want to provide angel funding for businesses starting in their state. One great way to find these funds is to contact your state's Department of Economic Development.

Angels tend to find most of their investment opportunities through friends and business associates, so whatever method you use to search for angels, it's also important to spread the word. Tell your professional advisors and people you meet at networking events, or anyone who could be a good source of referrals, that you're looking for investment capital. You never know what kind of people they know.

Be an angel and ask for the right amount of money when you do it.

5

VENTURE CAPITAL

MY GRANDFATHER USE to take me to a ball game every chance he got to visit with me. My favorite play in all baseball was when Freddy Potec sat in center field and waited for the pop fly to land in his glove. This chapter is about financial accuracy and having the knowledgeable experience to position yourself to make the catch.

Venture capital is the assets provided by external investors for financing startups, growing or struggling businesses. Venture capital investments generally are high- risk investments but offer the potential for above average returns. A venture capitalist (VC) is a person who makes such investments.

Who's Up to Bat?

A venture capital fund is a pooled investment vehicle (often a partnership) that primarily invests the financial capital of third-party investors in enterprises that are too risky for the standard capital markets or bank loans. Aspiring entrepreneurs looking to locate and secure venture capital have the option of seeking the support of a mentor capitalist. A mentor capitalist is an expert not only in acquiring capital but they can also provide support and direction to early start-ups.

Venture capital general partners (also known as "VCs") may be former chief executives at firms similar to those with the partnership funds. Investors in venture capital funds are typically large institutions with large amounts of pecuniary resources. Other positions at venture capital firms include venture partners and entrepreneur-in- residence (EIR).

Venture partners "bring in deals" and receive income only on deals they work on. EIRs are experts in a particular domain and perform due diligence on potential deals. EIRs are engaged by VC firms temporarily (six to eighteen months) and are expected to develop and pitch startup ideas to their host firm (although neither party is bound to work with each other).

Venture capital is not befitting for many entrepreneurs, because VCs are very selective in determining in what to invest. They are most interested in enterprises with high growth potential, as only such opportunities are likely capable of providing the financial returns and successful exit event within the required timeframe that venture capitalists expect. Because of these strict requirements, many entrepreneurs seek initial funding from angel investors—affluent individuals who dispense capital for business start-ups, usually in exchange for ownership equity.

The typical venture capital investment occurs after the seed funding[16] round as growth funding round (also referred to as Series A round) in the interest of generating a return through an eventual realization event, such as an IPO or trade sale of the company. Venture capital is a subset of private equity. Therefore, all venture capital is private equity, but not all private equity is venture capital.

In the Batter's Box

Within the venture capital industry, the general partners and other investment professionals of the venture capital firm are often referred to as venture capitalists or "VCs." Typical career backgrounds vary, but broadly speaking, venture capitalists come from either an operational or a finance background. Venture capitalists with an operational background tend to be former founders or executives of companies similar to those which the partnership finances or will have served as management consultants. Venture capitalists with finance backgrounds tend to have investment banking or other corporate finance experience.

Although the titles are not entirely uniform from firm to firm, other positions at venture capital firms include:
- *Venture partners* - Venture partners are expected to source potential investment opportunities ("bring in deals") and typically are compensated only for those deals with which they are involved.
- *Principal* -This is a mid-level investment professional position and is often considered a "partner-track" position. Principals

---

[16] Seed money refers to the money invested by one or more parties that have some connection to a new enterprise

- *Associate* - This is typically the most junior apprentice position within a venture capital firm. After a few successful years, an associate may move up to the "senior associate" position and potentially principal and beyond. Associates will often have worked for 1-2 years in another field, such as investment banking or management consulting.
- *Entrepreneur-in-residence* (EIR) - EIRs are experts in a particular domain and perform due diligence on potential deals. EIRs are engaged by venture capital firms temporarily (six to eighteen months) and are expected to develop and pitch startup ideas to their host firm, although neither party is bound to work with each other. Some EIRs move on to executive positions within a portfolio company. Venture capitalists are compensated through a combination of management fees and carried interest (often referred to as a "two and 20" arrangement):
- *Management fees* - an annual payment made by the investors in the fund to the fund's manager to pay for the private equity firm's investment operations.[17] In a typical venture capital fund, the general partners receive an annual management fee equal to up to 2% of the committed capital.
- *Carried interest* - a share of the profits of the fund (typically 20%), paid to the private equity funds management company as a performance incentive. The remaining 80% of the profits are paid to the fund's investors; strong limited partner interest in top-tier venture firms has led to a general trend toward terms more favorable to the venture partnership, and certain groups are able to command carried interest of 25-30% on their funds.

Because a fund may run out of capital prior to the end of its life, larger venture capital firms usually have several overlapping funds at the same time; doing so lets the larger firm keep specialists in all stages of the development of firms almost constantly engaged. Smaller firms tend to thrive or fail with their initial industry contacts. By the time the fund cashes out, an entirely new generation of technologies and people is ascending, whom the general partners may not know well, and so it is prudent to reassess and shift industries or personnel rather than simply attempt to invest more in the industry or people the partners already know.

---

[17] http://www.calpers.ca.gov/index.jsp?bc=/investments/assets/equities/aim/pe-glossary.xml

As an entrepreneur, you certainly understand the importance of business funding. Even if your business has yet to receive an influx of money, you undoubtedly have thought about the possibilities that such an influx would present. The question then is, what type of business funding should you look for. While there are many options available to you, venture capital funding may be one of your best choices.

This is because venture capital funding has some assumptions behind it. More often than not, venture capitalists have some sort of exit strategy. This means that they do not simply want to invest in companies for good will.

In most cases, they want one of two things:

1. A private sale of the company
2. To go public with the company

The reason for this is that these two exit strategies will give a company a high valuation. Often companies that go public sell for over ten times their actual worth. This is referred to a company's price-to-earnings ratio (PE ratio). The final result of venture capital funding could be that both the business founders and the venture capital funding company become rich.

Throwing the Right Pitch

Almost all Venture Capital investments in early stage technology and internet investments come down to just four key factors. And they're easy to remember because they all begin with positive motion, structural organization, long-range potential, and financial opportunity

1. Positive Motion. The most important factor that investors get their checkbooks out for is positive motion. Everyone has their own definition of energy (user numbers, revenue, channel partners, biz deals, whatever). You might hear, "We need to see some action." Really, this just means that they are not ready to invest in your company. Why? Chances are they don't know you well enough and can't judge your performance or capabilities. Some have "rules," but for the right reason they are willing to bend the rules.

Imagine the "typical" deal. A person walks into a VC's office, whom they have never met. He or she is highly referred by a friend and they are pitching a product demo with a power point presentation. With someone they have never met, they ask the potential investor to make a decision in two to three weeks because they are doing a road show.

That might work for $50-100k but less likely for $3M unless you are a seasoned entrepreneur, are known to the VC investor, have some metrics that work in your favor or have built something the VC believes to be truly unique. VC's are tough customers. They've "seen it all." This scenario is an example of a "brush-back" pitch. In baseball, it's a pitch thrown so far inside that it brushes back the batter. This is a common mistake when pitching a business or venture to a VC.

By placing an unrealistic timeframe for approval of funds or a commitment, it pushes back the investors. If I see your alpha product then I can judge how it develops over time. If you have two developers and the next time I see you it's a team of six with a new head of products, I can see positive motion. If you have beta customers, new pricing plans, different positioning, more market insights, good press coverage, these are all signs that the ball is moving forward. And that motion is easier to judge than a single data point.

Positive motion comes over time, and during that process, you build rapport with the investor. In almost every deal ever funded, time has allowed the investee to get to know the founders. To secure large sums, it will take time to build long-term relationships. During that process, the VC is looking for positive motion, signs of progression and developments.

2. Structural Organization. This is a no-brainer. Different VC's have different measuring points on the styles of management, product or product/market fit. Most VC's are 70 percent management and 30 percent product focused. But for any investor it takes a miracle to get investment dollars out of them if they're not impressed with the management team. You will find some investors who will say to themselves, "I could do this deal but the CEO will need to be replaced."

Most successful investors will not say that to you. Instead, if they get the feeling that the CEO can't cut it, most likely they will not invest. Never pitch without a plan. Pitch and plan are like movie and script: You don't do one without the other. The pitch summarizes the plan in a different medium. It's an output of the plan, optimized for the medium and the audience.

Because management is so important, the bio slide should be the first in your deck. If you have good experience then the VC will be leaning forward for the rest of the presentation. Having the right team—personnel who have credentials and experience—puts the odds in your favor.

3. Long-range Potential. Whether you're talking with micro VCs, seed stage investors, or series A, B investors, they all want to believe that your company can be big one day. They might want you to start lean. They might accept that a $50 million outcome will drive good returns given their small investment size, low price of entry, etc. However, almost all VCs care about investing in big markets with ambitious teams. So never talk about early exits, quick flips, tuck-in acquisitions, previous interest shown by acquirers, etc., during your meeting.

Instead, make sure you have a formula or some way of demonstrating why you believe this offers long-range potential. Don't kid yourself. You can't describe your business without knowing how much money you need, what you're going to spend it on and why. You have to define a target market and explain your rationale. You have to estimate sales and the cost of sales. You have to develop a strategic focus.

4. Financial Opportunity. The final factor is often misunderstood. Most VCs will want to be able to put a certain amount of money to work and will want to own a large enough percentage of your company to pay attention. There are modern investors who think differently and are willing to invest $100k as part of a $1.5 million round. But when they do it's just because they consider you part of their early stage investment portfolio where they're less sensitive about ownership percentage. If you "take off" they'll likely want to own more.

We can have an intellectual debate about whether it is the right investment strategy or not to have a minimum threshold. Most VCs want to own between 20-25 percent minimum of your company. If they co-invest with somebody else that they consider important, they might be willing to cut that back to 15 percent. Most VCs won't want to own eight percent of your company. If they do, it's probably because they want the option to invest more later.

When you "pitch" investors, for example, see it from their side. They're trying to guess the odds that a check they write tomorrow will generate lots of money in the near future. They want to know that you understand that. You talk about your management team because experience reduces risk. You talk about exit strategies because investors make nothing without the exit. You talk about market size, defensibility and scalability because that generates more money on exit. Way too many pitches just summarize the business, proudly, without focusing on what investors look for.

Understand the pitch as a medium. You do it for the viewing pleasure of the audience, not for yourself. It's about what they want, not what you want. You have to be inside their head, not your own. Call it empathy. Call it walking in their shoes or seeing things through their eyes.

Throwing the "right pitches" is not an attempt to "strike out" the investor. It's about letting them hit the ball—hit it out of the park. Keeping your presentation in the batter's box will increase your chances for the VC to want to play ball. When you learn to play ball, you will discover the benefits with teaming up with the right VCs, and experience the pleasure and privileges for success in business.

Play ball.

6

ECONOMIC INCENTIVES

THE USE OF ECONOMIC development incentives by states and localities to attract and retain businesses has become increasingly controversial. A few "mega projects," each involving a relatively large package of incentives distributed over a number of years, have received a great deal of publicity during the past decade. Yet, most state and local incentives are distributed through hundreds of small-scale programs and thousands of projects. As public sector budgets tighten and expectations rise among stakeholders, economic development policy makers and practitioners are seeking better tools to assess the impacts of these public investments. States and localities use economic development incentives to influence the location of business investments.

Direct distribution of public funds, through either reduced taxes or financial assistance, are the two most obvious ways for a state or local government to encourage economic development. As long as state and local tax structures and economic growth policies differ, these incentives will continue to be part of the economic development landscape.

A Better Way

Governors, mayors, legislators, and council members justify these public investments because private-sector decisions to invest in a community result in jobs, income, and tax revenues that are essential to the economic and social well-being of a community or state. Without these public investments, policy makers fear that they will not realize the level of private investment that the community or state might otherwise achieve. This will make the jurisdiction less competitive for current investments and begin a potential cycle of disinvestment as existing firms begin to find the community or state less viable economically. Many jurisdictions justify direct business assistance programs as strategies to overcome structural deficiencies in their state and local economic climates.

These incentives may also serve to upgrade human and physical capital in a community or region. For years' policy makers continued to support economic development programs, but recently the call for better analysis of the impacts of these incentives has increased for several reasons:

1. Increased use of economic development incentives has attracted the attention of legislatures, administrative agencies, and other groups to the cumulative costs of these programs.
2. Competition for public revenues within government, and among different governmental levels, has sparked interest in understanding the more precise costs and benefits of these programs.
3. The offering of incentives to large corporations, which are perceived as not really needing these benefits, has engendered an increasingly negative public view of these programs.
4. Poorly designed studies have inadequately defined the comprehensive fiscal and economic impacts of these programs on states and communities. Motivated by heightened media attention and academic research questioning the value of these programs, state and local policy makers have accelerated their search for ways to carefully examine more incentive investments.

Many public officials would prefer to reduce their dependence on these programs, yet most are unwilling to unilaterally set them aside, fearing a major loss of their competitive economic position relative to other states or communities.

Given these political realities, economic development professionals and policy makers require access to better tools for assessing the costs and benefits of these economic development incentives. In selecting an appropriate evaluation methodology, however, practitioners sometimes must wrestle with the need to assess the incentive awards as a way to achieve conflicting objectives: (1) satisfying myriad policy maker demands, and (2) guiding managers in the effective allocation of resources.

It is further complicated by evaluations, often conducted after the fact that may have a different view of a program's objectives than did the policy makers when they designed the program.

More and more, economic developers are recognizing the importance of using credible, objective methodologies for analyzing their investments in businesses. But several factors complicate the implementation of sound monitoring and evaluation principles. To respond more precisely to the needs of businesses, states and localities have become increasingly sophisticated in the variety of "incentive products" they offer.

Most states have developed detailed eligibility and targeting criteria, which guide the deployment of incentives. Yet much of the attention and criticism of incentive packages has been directed at "mega-projects," or those very large projects that require a packaging of incentives that must be approved by the state legislature.

A study, conducted in 1998 using the data on programs that provide a variety of incentive plans offered by states to support business investment and development identified three major categories of incentives: Direct financial incentives; indirect financial assistance; and tax-based incentives or rewards.

Direct Financial Incentives

Direct financial incentives are programs that provide direct monetary assistance to a business from the state or through a state-funded organization. The assistance is provided through grants, loans, equity investments, loan insurance and guarantees.

These programs generally address business financing needs but also may be invested in workforce training, market development, monetization, and technology commercialization activities. Cash grants provide the greatest flexibility and immediate benefit to the company by reducing capital outlays.

However, loans, bonds, and equity financing are commonly used to make resources available with an expectation that the dollars will be returned for future investments. Another important category of direct financial incentives is in the areas of training subsidies. Other forms of direct financial incentive include revolving loan funds, product development corporations, seed capital funds, and venture funds. These programs directly supplement market resources through public lending authorities and banks.

Indirect Incentives

Indirect incentives include grants and loans to local governments and community organizations to support business investment or development. The recipients include communities, financial institutions, universities, community colleges, training providers, venture capital investors, and childcare providers. In many cases, the funds are tied to one or more specific business location or expansion projects.

Other programs are targeted toward addressing the general needs of the business community, including infrastructure, technical training, new and improved highway access, airport expansions and other facilities. Funds are provided to the intermediaries in the form of grants, loans, and loan guarantees.

Indirect incentives may also be used to leverage private investment in economic development. For instance, linked deposit programs in which state funds are deposited in a financial institution in exchange for providing capital access or subsidized interest rates to qualified business borrowers.

Tax Incentives

We learned about tax credits and incentives in Chapter Three. Tax incentives are widely used as a strategy for leveraging business investments. States usually focus their incentives according to their tax codes, though many states stipulate local tax incentives that are designed to generate economic development. Tax credits provide a reduction in state income tax, franchise tax or other state taxes to reward businesses for a variety of behaviors such as creating jobs, investing capital in equipment or research and development, training workers, recycling, or providing childcare.

The Community Development Block Grant (CDBG), one of the longest-running programs of the U.S. Department of Housing and Urban Development, funds local community development activities such as affordable housing, anti-poverty programs, and infrastructure development.

CDBG, like other block grant programs, differs from categorical grants made for specific purposes in that they are subject to less federal oversight and are largely used at the discretion of the state and local governments and their sub grantees.

The CDBG provides funds for downtown revitalization, tourism, economic development, and public works, rebuilding urban regions and smaller communities.

Economic Development Association[18]

- Public Works and Economic Development
- Economic Adjustment Assistance (EAA)
- Planning
- Technical Assistance
- Research and Evaluation
- Trade Adjustment Assistance for Firms
- Community Trade Adjustment assistance
- Global Climate Change Mitigation Incentive Fund

Key Federal Funding Terms

Grants

Federal grants are funds which are provided to applicants through programs administered by one of 26 federal agencies. It is up to each agency to advertise and administer their programs, review applications, and choose grantees.

Project Grants

Project grants provide the funding—for fixed or known periods—of specific projects. Project grants can include fellowships, scholarships, research grants, training grants, trainees, experimental and demonstration grants, evaluation grants, planning grants, technical assistance grants, survey grants, and construction grants. Project grants can also be referred to as discretionary or categorical grants or funding.

Formula Grant

Formula grants are allocations of money to states or their subdivisions in accordance with distribution formulas prescribed by law or administrative regulation, for activities of a continuing nature not confined to a specific project.

---

[18] http://www.eda.gov/AboutEDA/Programs.xml

This includes Block Grants to states and local governments, which provide more leeway for states by providing funding for identified eligible activities.

Direct Loan

Lending of federal funds for a specific period of time, with a reasonable expectation of repayment; they may or may not require the payment of interest.

Guaranteed/Insured Loan

Programs in which the federal government makes an arrangement to indemnify a lender against part or all of any defaults by those responsible for repayment of loans.

Authorization

Authorization is the suggestion of funding levels for programs set by committees in Congress. Appropriations are the actual outlays of federal funds determined by the Appropriations Committees.

Appropriation

Appropriations are legislatively directed funds which are administered by federal agencies for general programs as well as specific projects. Programmatic funding is the general funding of an agency which is derived from Congress. Line Item Earmarks are the funding legislatively directed by Congress through Administrations for the purpose of specific projects.

Earmark

Essentially, an earmark is a congressionally directed grant that goes through the legislative process rather than the Administration. Each earmark must fit into a pre- existing congressionally authorized grant program and must adhere to the rules set out by the Administration for that grant program. They must also go through each agency's environmental review and auditing processes like any other federal grantee.

7

MICRO ENTERPRISES

M

THE Micro Enterprise…..

If your business is similar in size to 90% of businesses in the United States, it is considered a micro business or micro-enterprise.[19] And if you are searching for financing, a micro-enterprise loan might be the right financing tool for you! The definition of a micro business is one with ten (10) or fewer employees. For that reason, businesses are typically classified as "micro" when they start out. Sole proprietorships or self-employed businesses are known as micro businesses. Beyond the start-up phase, businesses may remain in the micro category as existing, ongoing, successful businesses. Some micro businesses emerge into high growth.

Micro businesses are found everywhere and represent every industry, including service, retail, wholesale or manufacturing. There are many resources available through micro-enterprise development organizations (MDOs) for micro businesses. Often a micro loan ($50,000 or less) provides part or most of the capital for a business to start or sometimes for its growth. A micro loan "fills a gap" in the financing plan; it may be combined with another capital source to meet the business's overall capital needs.

Why Serve Micro Businesses?

Micro businesses are the unsung heroes of the economy, both in the local community and at the state level. These businesses spend dollars locally and

---

[19] www.youreconomy.org: Overview - United States 2006 - 2008. Of over 23 million establishments in 2008 (economic business unit with a unique DUNS number), 35.3% were Self-Employed sole-proprietorships and 55.6% were considered Stage 1 businesses with 2 to 9 employees. For more information see also: http://youreconomy.org/pages/states/us.ye?region=Comp

have a personal stake in assuring that the community remains vibrant for future generations. Micro business owners or entrepreneurs are those that are active around their communities, volunteering in many capacities, and often times, if successful, they become the angel investors that can help others start businesses.

Entrepreneurs often become philanthropists that help build endowments to support community facilities and activities. Micro business owners exemplify the best of what the "good corporate citizen" model should be, and micro business owners also have an opportunity to build a personal asset base through business ownership.[20]

Micro-enterprise Development Organizations (MDOs) bring start-up and growing phase resources to micro businesses. MDO resources include loan capital, financial education, one-on-one technical assistance (business coaching/consulting), business management classes or various topics, as well as linkages to other resources, networking and peer learning opportunities. MDOs are generally nonprofit organizations with staff that understand the issues and challenges of the very smallest businesses, and most are experienced, credible lenders. A micro loan can offer a micro business owner a more personalized option in obtaining capital, which can be extremely valuable in the case of little or no business experience and lack of credit history or good credit in some cases.

What is a Micro Loan?

By current definition, a micro loan is generally considered a loan of $50,000 or less. In 2010, it was reported that micro loans to U.S. entrepreneurs averaged about $7,000.[21] Some MDO's help micro businesses by packaging loans that may include various lenders or business loan guarantees. In addition to MDOs, community revolving loan funds may provide micro size loans or larger. The micro loan might fill a financing gap. A loan package involving a micro loan can run as high as $200,000. With a combination of lenders involved in the loan package, the risk to any one lender is lowered.

Business owners often have a need for capital throughout the life of the business. In the start-up phase, they may have personal savings or support

---

[20] Public Sector Digest, Summer 2009, Micro-enterprise Development in Nebraska, Rose Jaspersen. www.publicsectordigest.com

[21] The Kiplinger Letters, November 18, 2010, Neema P. Roshania, Researcher-Reporter

from family, but all too often, they underestimate the total operating capital needed. As the business grows, there may be times when the cash flow needs an infusion of dollars during tight months.

Microfinance programs encourage micro business owners to visit with a local banker to seek traditional bank financing, and in some cases micro businesses may utilize the various financing methods described in this book.

Banks provide a tremendous service to the business community. They generally follow stringent loan underwriting protocols, considering the potential borrower's (business owner or entrepreneur) credit history, equity position, business experience and business plan. Banks often turn down financing requests especially with start-ups.

In times of economic uncertainty, traditional banks or lending institutions may tend to steer away from small business lending or they may tighten their credit standards. New business owners have often turned to credit card financing for small amounts of capital. With high interest rates on balances carried on credit cards, this type of financing is generally unsuitable as a long-term business financial solution.

When compared to credit card financing, micro- enterprise development organizations typically offer lower cost capital. However, these programs generally take on the riskier business financing deals that traditional financing institutions aren't doing, so their interest rates and charges often reflect added risk. In the last fiscal year, typical rates charged by MDOs in Nebraska[28] have been from 6% to 8% or three to five percentage points above the prime rate in the U.S. Nationally, rates can run much higher for micro loans, depending on the risk variables and amount borrowed. Micro loans are usually scheduled out for repayment over a fixed term, which is on average six years. However, the term may vary depending on the useful life of the collateral.

Many micro loan programs across the country are experienced and utilize some government funding or loans for their revolving capital. The SBA Micro Loan program helps fund about 180 organizations, all of which are screened for their ability to deliver services and loans effectively. Other government funding sources follow similar review procedures and certification processes, including the CDFI Fund and the U.S. Department of Treasury. These vetting processes include review of the loan program's lending policies and procedures and a review of the organization's staff and board to ensure that organizations utilizing their funds aren't doing so as predatory lenders.[29]

Some micro loan organizations provide loans nationwide. Work with micro lending organizations that serve your state or region first. Working with a lender that is focused on serving your community or region should pay benefits. Some of the personal interaction and one-on-one assistance will be lost if you work with a lender that has not established a physical presence near you.

Key factors in the micro loan application process:

1. Come ready to learn and be open about your needs as a potential or existing micro business owner. Take advantage of business training and/or one-on- one business coaching offered by micro lenders. Be ready to utilize and engage your micro loan consultant. Learn about the micro Lending organization, their loan policies and requirements.

2. Recent bankruptcies, current tax liens, judgments and unpaid loans must be addressed. These issues combined with unexplained poor credit history may prevent you from qualifying for a micro loan. Perfect credit isn't always needed. Weaknesses in your credit score may be offset by a strong business plan and loan application.

3. Demonstrate professionalism with a complete loan application. Character of the micro loan borrower is often a consideration. Provide good references and explain your past experiences and how you are prepared to start or advance your business.

4. Provide organized records of past income and expenses, recent tax returns along with projections of a positive cash flow that can show your ability to repay a micro loan. Provide complete financial statements, including a current balance sheet of the business and one for you personally.

5. Along with the loan application, provide a complete and detailed business plan.[22] Provide explanation on the need and expected uses for the micro loan funds that are requested.

6. Prepare a list of business or personal assets that can be used as collateral for a micro loan. If collateral is lacking, seek a co-borrower or co-signer that will support the loan. Describe what "skin you have in the game or your business". In order to make your business successful, what can you give up or sell? What do you have that you can borrow against in order to secure a business loan?

---

[22] Inc. Magazine, "How to Secure a Microloan", Elizabeth Wasserman, November, 2009, www.inc.com/secure-microloan_pagen_2.html

Important activities following receipt of a micro loan. Keep communication lines open with your micro lender. Keep your lender informed on any business changes or difficulties in your business. Continue to utilize their assistance. Most will work with you to help resolve issues if you have potential repayment problems. Borrowers must have deposits into the business bank account before payments are due. Traditional micro loans are generally loaned at a fixed rate over a fixed term with payments set up to automatically debit from your business bank account.

Micro lenders regularly report repayment experience with the three credit bureaus (TransUnion, Equifax, and Experian) and some utilize the services of Credit Builders Alliance, a nonprofit organization dedicated to helping non-traditional financial and asset building institutions serve their clients in building their credit and financial access in order to grow their businesses.

Successful repayment of micro loans, positive results and record keeping in your business may help you obtain traditional bank loans or other financing alternatives for your business in the future. It is the hope of many micro lenders that businesses graduate from their services and lending programs. Micro lenders want to see entrepreneurs flourish, businesses grow and continue adding employees/jobs and positively contribute to society and the economy ongoing.

In summary, here are some positive points about micro loans:

- Micro loans are smaller amounts of capital made available to match the current needs of micro businesses. They are often "prover" loans, so borrowers can advance to more traditional lending sources when more capital is needed for continued growth.
- Micro lenders often provide business plan counseling and help the business owner understand the use and management of business debt. Micro loan programs help borrowers connect with other business resources and networks to help benefit the business.
- Micro loans can help individual owners and businesses build business credit.
- Micro lenders often set requirements so owners who aren't able to obtain a loan from a bank or traditional source can obtain a loan from them.
- Micro loan repayment terms are similar to an installment note, with a set payment over a reasonable term.
- Micro loans can provide "gap" capital in participation with traditional lending sources to complete a loan package for micro businesses.

- Micro lenders and community development loan funds are available throughout the country. Utilize those organizations that specifically serve your area first.
- Here are some examples of micro-enterprise loans:

Example 1 - A young man just graduated from mechanized agriculture from a Midwest university. He came back to his rural community and together with his Dad started a design and manufacturing business where they make customized agriculture equipment. A micro loan of $40,000 and assistance with business planning was obtained through an area micro-enterprise development organization to help purchase their first two pieces of equipment used in the manufacturing process.

The business provided full-time employment for the young entrepreneur and his dad. With steady growth, the company has been able to hire additional workers each year. The company now has six employees and works directly with the local bank for its operating and expansion capital.

Example 2 - A single mother went back to school to become a massage therapist with an opportunity to join a salon operating her own micro business from that location. She needed $15,000 for initial financing to get started with inventory and supplies. The location was perfect and her business grew beyond her imagination. Within one year, she hired an office assistant with plans to rent additional space to add a partner therapist next year. Just $15,000 in micro financing helped kick-start this business to where she nets $65,000 per year and employs another person full-time in the business.

8

HOW TO GET A LOAN

L

IF YOU ARE A START-UP entrepreneur, getting a bank loan is like going through the eye of a needle. It is tough, but not completely impossible. You just need to do your homework well. Here are the kinds of preparation you will need to do in order to increase the chances of getting that bank loan approved.

Banks favor an established businessperson with a solid credit rating, a sizeable bank account, experience in the business they propose to enter, and business plans that show the ability to repay the loans. If you are not one, then you need to double your preparations to convince the banker to lend you that much needed start-up capital. If your business is a start-up, bankers will need to know as much as possible about you and your business. Lenders will ask an awful lot of questions, and it takes a great deal of work to put it all together.

However, many small business owners often make the mistake of not being adequately prepared when going to the bank to ask for the loan. Surprisingly, many loan applicants do not even have the slightest idea how or when they intend to repay the money they requested. Often they do not even know how much money they need. When asked how much money they want to borrow, many people give these two common responses: "How much money can I get?" and "As much as possible." Is it any wonder that lenders say no?

Preparation to Obtain a Loan

The bottom line is that it pays to do your homework before you ask for a loan. Bear in mind that the probability of getting your loan approved goes up if the degree of risk associated with lending you money goes down. To lower your risk and improve your odds of getting the loan, you need to anticipate the question lenders will ask you. You need to present your banker insights into your business that may enable him or her to approve your loan easily.

For example, prior to filling out a loan application, you should know:

> 1. Exactly how much money you need? Be as exact as possible, adding a little for contingencies and the unforeseen extra expenses.
> 2. How you plan to use the money? Telling the banker that you want a loan to "have working capital" to the fastest way for your loan to be denied. There are only three things you can do with a loan: buy new assets, pay off old debts, or to pay for operating expenses. Be as specific as possible.
> 3. How long it will take you to repay the loan? Your cash flow projections will help you formulate a repayment time frame for the loan. This is the time when you need to convince the banker of the good potential of your business and its long-term profitability.
> 4. What interest rate can you afford? There is no sense in tying yourself up in a loan that will squeeze out your profits and bleed your business dry. It does not benefit you to take on debt that cannot be repaid.
> 5. What can you use as security for the loan? A loan is a risk, and the bank needs to make sure that they can get their money back. You need to present your personal guarantee to repay the loan and collateral. Your goal is to convince the banker of the value of your collateral.

Of course, do not forget to present that all-important written business plan explaining in detail your business objectives, projected earnings for the next one to three years, marketing strategy, and other relevant information. Be sure your marketing strategies are outlined in detail to lend credence to your sales projections.

In addition to your business plan, you need to support your loan application with numbers—preferably good ones. Part of that homework is to gather the financial data that will enable you to prove to lenders that you are a good credit risk.

In short, this entails putting together a credit history that includes the following:

- Personal financial statement listing your assets and liabilities
- A list of all credit cards and their current balances
- All outstanding loans, including original balances, amounts outstanding, and current monthly payments
- Total monthly mortgage or rent payments
- Net monthly income from your home-based business, an outside job or other sources • Checking and savings account balances
- The value of your automobile(s), including original cost, balance owed, and current monthly payments
- The current value of all property, including real estate, stocks and bonds

Getting a loan is a hard road to travel. Bankers need to be sure that they are not taking inordinate risks with you. Your role as the loan applicant is to convince the bankers that you and your business are good credit risks.

Nevertheless, the banking industry has been the main source for lending in the U.S. for more the two hundred years. It is considered the classic form of financing, offering a wide array of services. Unlike SBA loans, the U.S. government does not guarantee commercial bank loans.

Obtaining a bank loan may be difficult since banks use different criteria when lending money, including the amount and purpose of the loan, company data (management and operations), the primary and secondary sources of repayment, financial statistics (balance sheets, cash-flow statements), credit history, etc.

First-time entrepreneurs may face several rejections from different banks before being approved. Don't get too discouraged because your loan request may not fit the loan portfolio of the bank. If you are turned down by a bank, try different ones.

For example, banks can only have a fixed percentage of their loans in certain categories, like commercial real estate. If you approach a bank that has reached their funding maximum for commercial real estate loans, you will be turned down. This is not because you did not qualify but because the bank could not make the loan. By approaching another bank, you may get approved.

Three Types of Financing with a Bank

In regards to financing, banks offer three primary services for obtaining financing for a business, Line of Credit, Term Loan and Intermediate Term Debt.

A *Line of Credit* is any credit source extended to a government, business or individual by a bank or other financial institution. A line of credit may take several forms, such as overdraft protection, demand loan, special purpose, export packing credit, term loan, discounting, purchase of commercial bills, etc.

Effectively, the line of credit is a bank account that can readily be tapped at the borrower's discretion. Interest is paid only on money actually withdrawn, although the borrower may be required to pay an unused line fee, often an annualized percentage fee on the money not withdrawn. Lines of credit can be secured by collateral or unsecured.[23] Revolving lines of credit are lines of credit that are granted to a business by a bank that is payable over the course of one year. This amount can be anywhere from $5,000 to $50,000. The entrepreneur can use the credit when needed and will be charged based upon what is used. In addition, the borrower's residential or commercial real estate serves as collateral.

A *Term Loan* is a loan from a bank for a specific amount that has a specified repayment schedule and a floating interest rate.[24] They typically carry fixed interest rates and monthly or quarterly repayment schedules and include a set maturity date.

Bankers tend to classify term loans into two categories:

- *Intermediate-term loans*: Usually running less than three years, these loans are generally repaid in monthly installments (sometimes with balloon payments) from a business's cash flow. According to the American Bankers Association, repayment is often tied directly to the useful life of the asset being financed.
- *Long-term loans:* These loans are commonly set for
more than three years. Most are between three and ten years, and some run for as long as twenty years. Long-term loans are collateralized by a business's assets and typically require quarterly or

---

[23] http://en.wikipedia.org/wiki/Line_of_credit
[24] http://www.investopedia.com/terms/t/termloan.asp#axzz1cR8jSHXU

monthly payments derived from profits or cash flow. These loans usually carry wording that limits the amount of additional financial commitments the business may take on (including other debts but also dividends or principals' salaries), and they sometimes require that a certain amount of profit be set aside to repay the loan.

These types of loans are primarily for the established small businesses that can leverage sound financial statements and substantial down payments to minimize monthly payments and total loan costs. Repayment is typically linked in some way to the item financed. Term loans require collateral and a relatively rigorous approval process, but they can help reduce risk by minimizing costs. Before deciding to finance equipment, borrowers should be sure they can they make full use of ownership-related benefits, such as depreciation, and should compare the cost with that of leasing.

In most cases, a business will visit a bank at some point in the process of its existence. Borrowing money from an outside source with the promise to return the principal, in addition to an agreed-upon level of interest, is the banks offer—*debt*. Although the term *"debt"* tends to have a negative connotation, startup companies commonly turn to debt to finance their operations. In fact, even the healthiest of corporate balance sheets will include some level of debt. In finance, debt is also referred to as "leverage." The most popular source for debt financing is the bank, but a private company or even a friend or family member can also issue debt.

Taking a loan is nothing new. Countless businesses have been set up on bank loans. Whether people take a loan for themselves or for their businesses, a bank loan is the most sought-after source of available financing. However, there are both advantages and disadvantages to taking a bank loan, depending on the borrower's financial health. This is why it is necessary to understand the pros and cons of bank loans before turning to them.

Advantages to Bank Financing

One advantage to bank financing is that you maintain ownership. When you borrow from the bank or another lender, you are obligated to make the agreed-upon payments on time. But that is the end of your obligation to the lender. You can choose to run your business however you choose, without outside interference.

Second, a huge attraction for debt financing is tax deductions. In most cases, the principal and interest payments on a business loan are classified as business expenses, and thus can be deducted from your business income taxes. It helps to think of the government as a "partner" in your business, with a 30 percent ownership stake (or whatever your business tax rate is).

If you can cut the government out of the equation, then it's beneficial to your business. Furthermore, you should analyze the impact of tax deductions on the bank interest rate. Banks that offer loans do so at competitive rates of interest and on mutually understood and accepted repayment terms, as compared to unconventional lenders. If a borrower meets the bank's lending criteria to the letter, he could benefit with a lower rate of interest and relaxed and easy repayment terms. Add to this the bonus of having a good working relationship with the bank.

Drawbacks to Bank Financing

As mentioned above, your sole obligation to the lender is to make your payments. Unfortunately, even if your business fails, you will still have to make these payments. In addition, if you are forced into bankruptcy, a bank will have claim to repayment before any equity investors. Often, loans come with a prepayment penalty, which prevents the borrower from paying the loan earlier than the stipulated date without incurring any extra costs.

Even after calculating the discounted interest rate from your tax deductions, as explained above, you may still be faced with a high interest rate. Interest rates will vary with macroeconomic conditions, your history with the banks, your business credit rating and your personal credit history.

It might seem attractive to keep bringing on debt when your firm needs money, a practice known as "levering up," but each loan will be noted and have an impact upon your credit rating. And the more you borrow, the higher the risk to the lender, and the higher interest rate you'll pay.

Even if you plan to use the loan to invest in an important asset, you will need to make sure your business will be generating sufficient cash flows by the time loan repayment starts. In addition, you will likely be asked to put up collateral on the loan in case you default on your payments.

There is always a chance of rejection when applying for any bank loan, especially if the business owners have poor credit history, little income, and no assets. There are other options to be explored, so don't throw in the towel too soon.

9

UNDERSTANDING SBA

EVERYONE HAS ENJOYED or heard of miniature golf. Can I Play Too?

Originally, the sport was designed for women in Scotland, in 1867. The story goes how women had become interested in the golf game, but the conservative social norms of that era deemed it unacceptable for women to publicly perform such violent movements that a golf swing requires.[25] Therefore, an 18-hole course of short putting greens was constructed for women, which was the first "miniature golf course" in the world.

A few decades later, it became customary for many American and British hotels to offer their guests a miniature-sized golf course, using the same designs as actual golf courses, but at one-tenth the scale. By the late 1920s, there were over 150 rooftop courses in New York City alone and tens of thousands across the United States.

The 18th and final holes of many miniature golf courses are designed to literally capture the ball, effectively preventing the player from playing additional rounds without purchasing another game. While the modern game of golf originated in 15th century Scotland, where the first written record of golf is James II's banning of the game in 1457 as an unwelcome distraction to learning archery.[26] To many golfers, the Old Course at St Andrews, a links course dating to before 1574, is considered to be a site of pilgrimage.[27]

Golf is documented as being played on Musselburgh Links, East Lothian, Scotland, as early as March 2, 1672, which is certified as the oldest golf course in the world by Guinness World Records. A typical golf course consists of 18 holes, but nine-hole courses are common and can be played twice through for a full round of 18 holes.[28] Early Scottish golf courses were

---

[25] http://www.terrastories.com/bearings/miniature-golf

[26] http://www.golf-information.info/history-of-golf.html

[27] Cochrane, Alistair (ed) Science and Golf IV: proceedings of the World Scientific Congress of Golf. Page 849. Routledge

[28] http://encarta.msn.com/encyclopedia_761570500/Golf.html#p2

primarily laid out on links land, soil-covered sand dunes directly inland from beaches.[29] This gave rise to the term "golf links," particularly applied to seaside courses and those built on naturally sandy soil inland. In 2008, the United States had 17,672 golf courses of the 35,112 courses worldwide, which makes up 50% of all courses in the world.[30]

Now you're probably wondering, where I am going with this, and what does miniature golf and the sport of golf have to do with financing a business or the Adopt A Model program. Well, in keeping with my style of writing and the same with my teaching, I think many times we complicate our explanations when it comes to economic strategies. I like to simplify terms and use comparison contrasts to illustrate definitions.

In my chronological evaluation of golf, we become consciously aware that the outdoor sport was initially designed for the rich and famous, wealthy country club colleagues, distinguishing affiliates of the royal family and influential members of society in Scotland. So distinguished by its participants the lower class was prohibited and women were banished from the sport.

Elite golf courses erected, demonstrating prestigious greens and fairways amongst gorgeous landscaping, stunning views and premium water designs. With high priced memberships and expensive greens fees, only the "who's who" shared the status and privileges to play 18 rounds on the finest courses. Miniature golf was erected to suffice the desires of the less fortunate who were determined to enjoy the game. Those who wanted to play the prestigious sport found "putt-putt" to meet their requirements for 18-holes of golf. On a smaller scale, and over time, the miniature game became very popular and afforded everyone the opportunity to participate in the entertainment.

Leveling the Playing Ground

The same could be said regarding the participation of financing, loans, and investment opportunities. Seldom, if ever, do the rich or wealthy executives receive a declined notice when it comes to a loan or to borrowing funds for business development or economic growth. For too long, regulations, status and biased judgment prevented the local businessperson from obtaining a loan. The small business, the individual who is motivated by a dream, idea, invention and a product or service that could produce a

---

[29] http://www.etymonline.com/index.php?search=links&searchmode=none
[30] http://en.wikipedia.org/wiki/Golf#cite_note-31

beneficial commodity to consumers and at the same time, stir trade and industrial growth and economic development could not participate.

Years ago, local families ran banks. Getting a loan was as simple as a handshake. But during the post- World War era, and after the Korean War, local business was not expanding. And by the late 70s, local banks were being bought out and managed by corporate executives in other states, and the day of the small town business model was quickly replaced with bureaucracy. The small business owner saw a great divide between the wealthy and the middle class. He was no longer able to reserve a spot (at the local bank) or on the preverbal 18-hole country club golf course.

The small business owner needed a "miniature golf" course to even the playing field. For business owners and up-and-coming entrepreneurs, their miniature golf course would come in a small package—providing the same services, but on a smaller scale. It is called the Small Business Administration (SBA). The (SBA) is a United States government agency that provides support to entrepreneurs and small businesses. President Eisenhower, with the signing of the Small

Business Act, created the SBA on July 30, 1953. Its function was and is to "aid, counsel, assist and protect, insofar as is possible, the interests of small business concerns."

The mission of the Small Business Administration is "to maintain and strengthen the nation's economy by enabling the establishment and viability of small businesses and by assisting in the economic recovery of communities after disasters."

Par for the Course

The most visible elements of the SBA are the loan programs it administers. The SBA does not provide grants or direct loans—with the exception of Disaster Relief Loans. Instead, the SBA guarantees against default, certain portions of business loans made by banks and other lenders that conform to its guidelines.

One of the most popular uses of SBA loans is commercial mortgages on buildings occupied or to be occupied by a small business. These programs are beneficial to small businesses because most bank programs frequently require larger down payments and/or have repayment terms requiring borrowers to refinance every five years. They can be beneficial to the bank in that banks can reduce risk by taking a first-lien position for a smaller percentage of the project, then arranging for a SBA Certified Development Company to finance the remainder through a second-lien position.

The SBA provides services for a small business to obtain financing through four programs.

- The first is the 7(a) Loan Guarantee Program. It is designed to help small entrepreneurs start or expand their businesses. The program makes capital available to small businesses through bank and non-bank lending institutions. The Small Business Jobs Act of 2010 permanently increased the maximum size of these loans from $2 million to $5 million.
- Second, the Fixed Asset Financing Program is administered through non-profit Certified Development Companies throughout the country. This program provides funding for the purchase or construction of real estate and/or the purchase of business equipment/machinery.
- Third, the Microloan Program instituted through the Small Business Jobs Act increased the maximum amount of SBA microloans from $35,000 to $50,000. These are offered through non-profit microloan financial intermediaries.
- Finally, the fourth program is the Disaster Assistance Loan, which assists homeowners and renters who are eligible for long-term, low-interest loans to rebuild or repair a damaged property to pre-disaster condition.

Businesses are also eligible for long-term, low-interest loans to recover from declared disasters. Allow me to highlight that if a business with a Disaster Relief Loan defaults on the loan, and the business is closed, the SBA will pursue the business owner to liquidate all personal assets to satisfy an outstanding balance.

In addition to the four standard loan programs, there are two specialized programs. The first is the 8(a) Business Development Program, which assists in the development of small businesses owned and operated by individuals who are socially and economically disadvantaged, such as women and minorities. The second program is an SBA program for small companies that operate and employ people in Historically Underutilized Business Zones, thus, it is called the HUB Zone program.

10

EQUIPMENT LEASING

EVERY TIME I MEET with city officials or the chamber of commerce in rural communities, especially in the Midwest, where I live, I am often asked how I can help local construction companies or farmers with getting better equipment for their businesses or farms. The need for equipment and machinery are often the greatest challenge for small businesses, especially when they are competing with large corporations. Without the proper tools, technology and equipment, today's small businesses and farmers don't stand a chance.

When my son was small, I never objected to him watching the television program, Bob the Builder. This British children's animated television show broadcasts in many countries but originates from the United Kingdom. In the original series Bob appears as a building contractor specializing in masonry in an animated program with his colleague Wendy, various neighbors and friends, and their gang of toy figures who work vehicles and equipment (all made of clay).

Can You Fix It?

In each episode, Bob and his gang help with renovations, construction, and repairs and with other projects as needed. The show emphasizes conflict resolution, co-operation, socialization and various learning skills. Bob's catchphrase is "Can we fix it?" to which the other characters respond with "Yes, we can!" In most rural American regions, the question most asked by local communities to their local construction and builders is, "Can you fix it"? and the answer is, "No, we can't." Why? Because they don't have the necessary equipment to do the job, reasonably, affordably, and practically.

What's the answer?

When Bob the builder didn't have a tool, or a piece of machinery broke down on the job, the plot always showed teamwork and sharing as the option to solving the problem. In a sense, Bob leased equipment to get the job done. So can you. This brings me to one of the easiest ways to increase business, boost job growth and create a sustainable ecosystem for financial development—equipment loans.

Equipment loans are used to finance business vehicles, tools, fixed assets, and large computer systems. The equipment can be new or used. If new equipment, the loan can be for the total amount of the purchase. Used equipment is often 75% of the current cost of the equipment. It is easier to finance equipment that has a strong resale market (such as trucks and construction equipment) than specialized equipment with little resale use.

Even though the equipment will be used as collateral, borrowers still need to show they can repay the loan. You may need to provide business financial statements and business tax returns. Most times, borrowers may be required to personally guarantee the loan.

What are the Differences Between a Lease and a Loan?

Equipment loans and equipment leases are different. In an equipment loan, the loan requires the end user to invest a down payment in the equipment. The loan finances the remaining amount. The end user bears all the risk of equipment devaluation because of new technology.

End users may claim a tax deduction for a portion of the loan payment as interest and for depreciation, which is tied to IRS depreciation schedules. Financial accounting standards require owned equipment to appear as an asset with a corresponding liability on the balance sheet. A larger portion of the financial obligation is paid in today's dollars that are more expensive. At the end of a loan, you own the equipment. At the end of a lease, you can return the equipment and presumably start the lease process again.

For bookkeeping purposes, if you have a loan, you put the asset and loan on your balance sheet. If you have a lease, you do not put them on your balance sheet; the lease payments are strictly operating expenses. In both cases, if you don't make payments, the lender (or leaseholder) will repossess the equipment.

When using an equipment lease, the lease finances only the value of the equipment expected to be depleted during the lease term. The lessee usually has an option to buy the equipment for its remaining value at the end of the lease. The end user transfers all risk of obsolescence to the lessor, as there is no obligation to purchase the equipment at the end of the lease.

When leases are structured as true leases (operating leases), the end user may claim the entire lease payment as a tax deduction. The equipment write-off is tied to the lease term, which can be shorter than IRS depreciation schedules, resulting in larger tax deductions each year. The deduction is also the same every year, which simplifies budgeting. Note that equipment financed with a conditional sale lease, like a $1 buy-out, is treated the same as owned equipment and is called a capital lease.[31]

Leased assets are expensed when the lease is an operating lease. Such assets do not appear on the balance sheet, which can improve financial ratios. More of the cash flow, especially the option to purchase the equipment, occurs later in the lease term when inflation makes dollars cheaper.

Equipment Leasing Options

There are different levels and types of leasing. Small leases are typically under $20,000. There are a whole set of lenders who focus in this space only. Leasing can be more risky in this space because the folks usually have weaker credit. Commercial leases are those that are above $50,000. Clients are typically more stable and fees are usually smaller. Technology leasing is a program designed for PCs and laptops.[32] These leases only last two to three years.

Choosing to lease is a smart way to acquire equipment. By signing a lease, the lessee assigns his or her purchase rights to the lessor, who already owns or who then buys the equipment as specified by the lessee. When the equipment is delivered, the lessee formally accepts it and makes sure it meets all specifications. The lessor pays for the equipment, and the lease takes effect.

---

[31] http://www.thinkreelgreen.com/lease-glossary.html
[32] http://goliath.ecnext.com/coms2/gi_0199-12661625/Businesses-of-ll-Sizes-Look.html

Benefits of Leasing

Leasing offers numerous advantages over other financing methods.

First, there are tax deductions. There are both capital and operating leases.[33] The IRS does not consider an operating lease to be a purchase, but rather a tax-deductible overhead expense, where the lease amount can be deducted on a monthly basis. Therefore, you can deduct the lease payments from your corporate income.

The second benefit is balance sheet management. Because an operating lease is not considered a long-term debt or liability, it won't appear as debt on your financial statement; this is called an off-balance sheet transaction. Because the lease doesn't show up on your balance sheet, you are more attractive to institutional lenders, like banks, when you need them.

The third benefit is 100 percent financing. With leasing, there is very little money down, perhaps only the first and last month's payment are due at the time of the lease. Since a lease does not require a down payment, it is equivalent to 100 percent financing. That means that you will have more money to invest in revenue-generating activities.[34]

The fourth benefit is immediate write-off of the dollars spent. Lease payments are treated as expenses on a company's balance sheet; therefore, equipment does not have to be depreciated, and you, in essence, get accelerated depreciation.[35]

The fifth benefit is flexibility. As your business grows and your needs change, you can add or upgrade at any point during the lease term through add-on or master leases. If you anticipate growth, be sure to negotiate that option when you structure your lease program. You also have the option to include installation, maintenance and other services, if needed.[36]

The sixth benefit is customized solutions. A variety of leasing

---

[33] http://www.leasingideas.com/leasing-benefits.html
[34] http://www.healthleadersmedia.com/page-1/FIN-268988/12-Benefits-of-Leasing-Equipment
[35] http://www.forbes.com/2007/01/24/smallbusiness-equipmentlease-IRS-ent-fin-cx_nl_0124nolo.html
[36] http://ezinearticles.com/?Benefits-of-Leasing-Equipment&id=187394

products is available, allowing you to tailor a program to fit your month-to-month or year-to-year cash flow needs. You are able to customize a program to address your needs and requirements—cash flow, budget, transaction structure, cyclical fluctuations, etc. Some leases allow you, for example, to miss one or more payment without a penalty, an important feature for seasonal businesses.[37]

The seventh benefit is asset management. A lease provides the use of equipment for specific periods at fixed payments. The lessor assumes and manages the risk of equipment ownership. At the end of the lease, the lessor is responsible for the disposition of the asset.[38]

The eighth benefit is upgraded technology. If the nature of your industry demands that you have the latest technology, a short-term operating lease can help you get the equipment and keep your cash. Lease equipment that you expect to depreciate quickly. Your risk of being caught with obsolete equipment is lower because you can upgrade or add equipment to meet your ever-changing needs.[39]

The ninth benefit is speed. Leasing can allow you to respond quickly to new opportunities with minimal documentation and red tape. Many leasing companies can approve your application within one or two days and you can have your equipment very quickly.[40]

Finally, the tenth benefit is cash advantages:
    a. Improved cash forecasting. By leasing equipment, you know the amount and number of lease payments over the life of the leasing period, so you can accurately forecast cash requirements for your equipment.
    b. Flexible end of term options. There are several options for disposing of equipment after the lease term ends, including returning the equipment, renewing the lease or purchasing the equipment.
    c. Tax benefits. Lessors often pass the tax benefits of ownership on to the lessee in the form of lower monthly payments.
    d. Improved earnings. Operating lease accounting provides a lower cost than a capital lease in the early years of a

---

[37] http://www.bizhelp24.com/money/business-finance/leasing-in-business-advantages-disadvantages.html
[38] http://www.kefonline.com/Downloads/PDF/KEF-HealthLeaders-July2011.pdf
[39] http://www.allbusiness.com/business-finance/leasing-office-l asing/1013-1.html
[40] http://www.kefonline.com/Downloads/PDF/KEF-HealthLeaders-July2011.pdf

lease.[41]

What Types of Companies Lease?

Lessees vary widely from small, one-person operations to Fortune 100 corporations, and the kinds of equipment being leased are just as diverse. Transactions range from a few thousand dollars' worth of equipment (such as fax machines) to multi-million dollar cogeneration facilities, telecommunications systems, medical equipment (including CAT scanners and MRI imaging), office systems, computers, commercial airliners, and transportation fleets.

Evaluate Your Financing Options

A lease is a financing agreement that is structured to meet your organization's special needs. To decide if leasing is the best option in your case, you must first understand those needs and ask yourself these questions:

- How does this equipment make my business more competitive?
- What is the most efficient use of my cash flow to pay for this equipment?
- How long will I use it?
- What will my equipment needs be in the future?

Obviously, you will want to factor the cost of leasing into your evaluation. Generally, the cost of leasing is comparable to those of other financing options when looking at the whole transaction. It is important to point out that leases are not loans. As a result, their costs are figured differently from those of loans.

Leases take into account that the equipment is worth something at the end of the lease term. This is called its residual. Residuals are built into lease pricing, usually making the lease payments lower than a loan. To compare lease products, it is better to compare monthly payments than to try to

---

[41] http://ezinearticles.com/?Benefits-of-Leasing-Equipment&id=187394

compare loan interest rates with lease rates. On a cost-of-capital basis, leasing may be the least expensive option.

Leasing companies can offer competitive rates for a number of reasons. Lessors with their volume purchasing power can secure attractive financing deals and pass along the savings to the lessee. The lessor also is better able to take advantage of the deduction for depreciation expense that comes with ownership.

Once you have completed your evaluation and decided to lease your next equipment acquisition, the first step is to select the type of lease that fits your needs. There are several different types of leases. You and your lessor should consider these factors in determining which is best for you:

- How long you want to use the equipment?
- What you intend to do with the equipment at the end of your lease?
- What is your tax situation?
- What is your cash flow?
- What are your company's specific needs as they relate to future growth?

You also will need to determine what happens at the end of the lease. Your options can include returning the equipment to the lessor, purchasing the equipment at fair market value for a nominal fixed price, or renewing your lease.

Technology Rotation Leasing

In the past decade, the rate of obsolescence has accelerated in the technology sector. As a result, computer hardware and software becomes outdated in months, instead of years. Even networked office equipment and peripherals can create an archaic feel to even the most innovative business.

The Technology Rotation Lease not only provides businesses with the means to acquire the technology they need, it provides you with an opportunity to generate more leasing business. And at the same time, you're able to bring greater value to the relationships you enjoy with your customers.

It's a well-known fact that companies that are interested in maintaining a progressive position in their markets refresh their desktop technology every two-to- three years.[42] Through the Technology Rotation Lease, brokers are able to compete with the national companies and provide the service mid-sized companies are looking for.[43]

Flexible lease terms from 24 to 36 months leases provide true technology rotation that enables clients to benefit from the equipment during its most useful life, then update as new technology becomes available. In addition, it creates a cycle that helps you to build more profitable, ongoing relationships.

A Fair Market Value Lease can be used to cycle your equipment every two to three years, depending on your needs. One scenario is to replace half of the machines in year one on a two year lease, and repeat the process the following year. Other scenarios include lease schedules as needed—monthly schedules, quarterly, or annually. Fair Market Value Leases allow businesses to stay on the cutting edge with minimal capital outlays.[44]

How do you know if you would benefit from technology rotation?

Consider these questions:

- ✓ Will your company need technology replacement according to the standard industry life cycle?
- ✓ Do you have a business need for rapid technological change?
- ✓ Is there a business need for quick adoption of new technologies?
- ✓ Have you evaluated your software needs?
- ✓ Will you need higher end software users with frequent software upgrades?

Other benefits for technology rotation are that it helps with disposal of old assets. It helps cut down costs in years four and five (i.e., memory upgrades). It provides cash flow assistance. And, it solves the problem of obsolescence.

---

[42] http://firststarcapital.net/programs_technology.html

[43] http://cityskywallpaper.blogspot.com/2009/03/businesses-of-all-sizes-look-to-leasing.html

[44] http://vicapital.com/Technologrotation.html

Typical Programs

1. Specific programs:
2. Laptop programs. The main reason people are leasing laptops is because battery life and wear and tear after two years. A typical lease for laptops is a 24-month rotation schedule.[45]
3. Desktops leases are usually on a 36-month program. Some leases are shorter term, but the value and cost savings in rotating their equipment is a great option.

The best fit for the Technology Rotation Lease are the companies who use what we define as Tier 1 equipment like DELL[46] and HP.[47]

The following are questions regarding the Technology Rotation Lease:

How much does it cost to return the equipment at the end of the lease?

Companies don't charge you for returning the equipment at the end of the lease. So your expenditure is whatever it cost to ship it back to the leasing company. Most companies don't expect you to return the equipment in the original boxes, but rather ask that it is returned in good condition.

What if I want to buy some of the equipment and return the rest?

That's okay, as long as expectations are set regarding what equipment is being returned. They will quote fair market value of the equipment you are keeping and you return the rest.

What about renewal?

Options offered include a month-to-month lease. Near the end of your lease, leasing companies contact you to determine what your intentions are, and in most cases, try to get you to purchase upgraded equipment or sell you the equipment at a fair value. You may either continue to rent, buy some of the equipment and return the rest, or return all the equipment.

---

[45] http://www.techrepublic.com/article/buy-or-lease-members-sound-off-about-stretching-the-life-cycles-of-pcs/1039336

[46] http://www.thefreelibrary.com/Dell+Offers+Zero-Percent+Thirty Month+Lease%3B+Low,+Fixed+Monthly...-a0116191810

[47] http://firststarcapital.net/programs_technology.html

Are the leases drawn up as an Operating Lease?
Since there is no collateral, the financing cannot be an operating lease.

Are the lease payments 100% deductible on tax returns as are true Operating Leases?
The payments are 100% deductible and can often be expensed in the current year. Clients are advised to seek advice from their tax professional, as tax situations vary.

Are challenged credits and start-ups acceptable if so, what is the minimum acceptable FICO score?
Challenged credits are acceptable. Although there is no hard minimum FICO score, 600 is a good benchmark. Underwriters look at other variables such as Time in Business (TIB), nature of business, home ownership, item being lease-financed, etc.

If more than one owner, do all owners have to sign the application and have FICO scores that meet the minimum, or can one owner with good scores carry the deal?
All owners must sign. The lenders look at the overall picture, not just individuals.

Are Co-Signers with good credit allowed, and if so, does the Co-Signer have to be a family member, or can a friend Co-Sign?
Co-signers may help strengthen the deal, and they do need to be an immediate family member.

Are start-up businesses (no TIB) acceptable, and does that client have to be a homeowner?
Start-up businesses are acceptable and being a homeowner does help a great deal.

Is there a requirement for a Loss-Payee Insurance Certificate to add the funder as an Additional Insured?
The lender must be added to the Lessee's insurance and listed as loss-payee and as additional insured. If the Lessee does not have insurance, most leasing companies offer it as a benefit to them and to you.

What Can Be Leased?

There is equipment that can be leased for virtually every industry sector that conducts business, such as:

Amusement equipment	**Medical Equipment**
Arcade games	Blood Analyzers
Gaming Machines	CT Scanners Exam Tables
Jukeboxes Pool tables Simulators	Dental Equipment
	Heart Monitors
Banking	Lab Testing Equipment
ATMs	Optical Equipment
Check Scanners	Physical Therapy X-ray
Sorters	Equipment
Encoders	
	Mining, Oil and Gas Extraction
Computers	Blast hole drills
CAD/CAM systems	Concrete transit machinery
File Servers	Draglines
Hardware	Electric and hydraulic shovels
Macro-computers	Extraction machinery
Mainframes	Loaders
Micro-computers	Pumps
PC Network	
Peripherals	**Office Equipment**
Plotters Printers Scanners	Copiers
Software	Embossers/Folders
Workstations	Facsimile Equipment
	File Cabinets
Construction	Furniture
Bulldozers	Labeling Machines Postage
Cement trucks	Machines
Compactors	Telephones
Concrete equipment	
Cranes	**Printing/Publishing**
Earth moving equipment	Binders/Cutters
Excavators	Colorimeters
Jackhammers	Computerized Press
Portable construction lighting	Equipment

Shovels
Surveying equipment

Electrical
AC Motors DC Motors Generators
Lighting equipment
Single & Three Phase motors
Transformers
Welders

Industrial and Manufacturing
Grinders
Lathes
Material handling machines
Packaging equipment Production
Equipment Punch/Press
Machines
Welding Equipment
Silkscreen Equipment
Injection Molding Machinery
Sewing/Embroidery/
Material Handling Equipment
Forklifts
Pallet Jacks
Platform Lifts
Conveyers

Live stock
Agricultural, Forestry,
Fishing Equipment
Harvesting and Planting Hay and
Cotton Bailers
Tractors
Dairy Machinery Food Processing
Tractors

Graphic Cameras Photo
Processing
Equipment
Printing Presses
Typesetting Equipment

Restaurant Equipment
Bar equipment
Countertop griddles
Electric Slicers Food warmers
Fryers
Furniture
Glo-Lite Signs
Grills
Hot Dog equipment
Ice Machines
Microwaves
Paging Systems Popcorn Makers

Transportation
Aircraft
Buses
Containers
Fresh/Saltwater Garbage Trucks
Passenger Vans
Tow Trucks
Railroad Trailers Trucks

Vending
Candy/Snack machines
Change machines
Soft drink dispensers

11

Financial Inclusion

CONGRESS APPROVED the Jumpstart Our Business Startups Act in the summer of 2012—A door of opportunity for those trying to raise alternative capital. This micro finance solution for the small business environment is definitely going to be a catalyst in the alternative finance movement.

One of the micro lending solutions under the ACT was the crowdfunding provision policy. Under the crowdfunding provision of the law, which was one of several major changes to longstanding securities laws, companies are permitted to raise up to a million dollars from the public through new online funding portals. For the time being, entrepreneurs can offer equity deals through the portals only to accredited investors; others can contribute to crowdfunding campaigns only in exchange for gifts, not an equity stake in the venture.

For the SEC, the challenge in drafting the specific rules has been a semantic challenge at best to get the right balance between protecting non-accredited (often less wealthy and less seasoned) investors from shady offerings, while still stripping away barriers to capital for entrepreneurs.

When the rules were proposed in fall of 2014, an incredible response made way to a gain in traction. Securities and Exchange Commission Chair Mary Jo White said in 2014 that issuing final crowdfunding rules would be a priority. More than a year later, it appears the wait will now continue into 2015. (Jonathan Ernst/Reuters). Crowdfunding is an avenue for entrepreneurs, startups and SMBs to solicit Working Capital from non-accredited investors.

The Crowdfunding provisions of the JOBS Act (H.R. 3606 Jump Start Our Business Startups Act) allows companies to raise up to $1 million in capital per year through crowdfunding platforms from individual investors without the requirements to register with the SEC (Securities and Exchange Commission). Many investors will come from family, friends, venture capitalists, entrepreneurs' preexisting networks, mentors, and former colleagues.

Clearly, there are many unknowns as the SEC completes the development of the functional details and related regulations of Crowdfunding Platforms hopefully a whopping two years later. However, there are many steps that small businesses can take to get ready.

You need two to four months of planning and preparation ahead of a Crowdfunding campaign to:

- Build and develop your business concept and your "business plan."
- Build your Crowd and your Social Capital Engines. •Build your virtual office, communication and collaboration suite in the cloud (web 2.0).
- Start building the "Crowd" as early as possible for your "crowd" funding campaign. As you see, Crowd comes first before funding.
- Protect your idea while your project is posted in Crowdfunding campaign for all the world to see.

One answer might be to file a "provisional patent application" as soon as possible. More and more businesses and individuals are turning away from banks and towards this form of alternative financing, and providers, both peer-to-peer lenders, like crowdfunding platforms. Crowdfunding is growing around the world by no less than 150% a year.

This 2017 will bring more growth, but it'll also have surprises. A high-profile crowdfunded project will fail, a peer- to-peer lending platform will deliver disappointing returns to donors, or a smaller platform will go under, taking people's money with it. Quakle, an early peer-to-peer lending platform, went under back in 2012. We've already seen some hindsight trivia of this.

Some crowdfunding donors were riled when crowdfunded pioneers of Oculus were sold to Facebook for billions but the donors received zero return. When the price of Bitcoin plummeted this year, there were stories of naïve investors who'd put their life savings into it and were burnt. And there have already been calls for the regulators of crowdfunding platforms to prevent consumer fraud claims. So when you present your company in the Alternative funding arena, remember that it is a risk for people to invest in you, and you should do everything you can to secure and encourage a viable opportunity.

Right now, alternative finance is a niche but soon to be a standard practice in the business funding landscape. And sometimes, investments don't work out. Projects fail, borrowers can't repay their loans, stuff happens. Some element of risk is an inherent part of finance.

The World Bank commissioned a study on crowdfunding in 2013 and found that the market has the potential to grow in 2025 by $90 billion. By channeling capital directly into structures like crowdfundingamerica.org, smallbusinesscrowdfunding.org, and constructioncrowdfunding.org, investors allow companies to raise money in a cost-effective and compliant manner.

I do not want to scare you but inform you. Crowdfunding is becoming an increasingly popular way for startup businesses and more mature firms to raise money. Of course, raising money for your business through crowdfunding isn't that easy. It is not as simple as it sounds and requires strategic provisions.

How to raise money by rewards-based crowdfunding Platforms.

It sounds easy: post your funding needs up on a website, offer some small rewards, and viola, you're on your way to fundraising. Of course, it's not that easy or everyone would do it.

Here's how it works for Fundraising and Investing

REWARD FUNDING

Giving the right reward and the right incentive can be the difference between obtaining your funding goals and missing them. So create tiered reward programs for smaller donations ($5-$50) and larger ones ($50+). Get inside your donors' heads and figure out what's going to motivate them without developing insecure doubts.

Post your campaign to one of our crowdfunding platforms: prepare your materials, a sweet video and your rewards, and publish them on the crowdfunding platform we   offer with your free membership. It's really important not to rely on your platform of choice for bringing in your donors. Research has shown that there's a direct correlation to the strength of your social media work sharing with your social networks and success in crowdfunding. Take in your money and get ready to deliver the rewards: If you hit your target, you'll receive your money.

Crowdfunding in the good

The possible good: using rewards-based crowdfunding you're raising money for your project or business without selling off an equity stake in your business. These are donations. You can get one or thousands of people committed to the success of your campaign. In some way, this type of crowdfunding takes all the risk out of the financing of building a new product. Instead of paying to create something fresh, crowdfunding donors will pay you to create it (in return for a reward or incentive).

Crowdfunding in the possible bad

Once you've successfully raised money, you've got to ship whatever you're producing. The demand in your fund raising promises if not met will damage your integrity very quickly if not delivered. Because of the binary nature of some crowdfunding campaigns (if you don't hit your target, you get nothing), it's potentially a lot of work running a campaign that ultimately fails.

Equity crowdfunding

As opposed to rewards-based crowdfunding where funding comes in the form of donations for a reward, equity crowdfunding means you're raising money by selling off a piece of your company. By taking angel investing online, equity crowdfunding has opened up this type of investing to more and more people.

There are very accomplished investors using these platforms, whose contribution could add to the success of a business long term. Managing numerous investors in your company becomes a very time-consuming job. Instead of raising money from numerous investors, some equity crowdfunding platforms pool the funds they raise into a single investment, making one point of contact for reporting requirements.

Getting comfortable with equity crowdfunding means you must get comfortable with increased transparency into your business.

Why give away a piece of your company if you could receive donations to build your next killer product? Giving away a piece of your business' equity will only benefit you if you're getting something valuable in return (like the participation of experienced investors in your industry, for example).

Be a crowdfunding investor

The middle class can now invest that extra $150 dollars a month and get a decent return using this alternative investment model. The crowdfunding model is not just for raising capital but for investing it. Some companies only need $10,000.00 to expand their company. If twenty neighbors all gave $500, they would each have a possible $75.00 a month coming in for the next three years, depending on the ROI agreement.

CONCLUSION

Start Up 101 is to equip you with the knowledge to start right. How you start is how you will finish. I hope these resources will encourage you for the next steps in your journey.

Remember to only make decisions that fit in the family plan instead of fitting the family in the business plan. What you see is what you are looking for. Please feel free to share this book with your family and friends.

Fredrick Hiner

STARTUP 101

The US Small Business Association's $24.2 Billion Bad Loan Portfolio sure does not help out the economy or small business Industry. It is hard enough to get funded let alone be on the back end of those who went before us, and screwed up financial opportunities we might have otherwise qualified for.

If you are starting a business and do not want to be apart of the 90% failure rate statistic, then you better have some resources in your tool box to be competitive enough to beat the odds.

This book will provide some of the most viable resources to help you sustain a legacy for your family. How you start is how you will finish. STARTUP 101 has the answers you need.

FREDRICK HINER

is 100% a family man who almost lost his family because of a start up business gone wrong.

Mr. Hiner started a 200 million dollar business and lost it in the recession. That loss, opened his eyes to a whole new world of business.

"It is not what you see and know that can steal your legacy, it is what you do not know and can not see that is the biggest thief in small business failure."

Mr. Hiner wrote this book to help prepare you before you start a new business. The resources in this book will help protect your family from financial harm if you use it.

ISBN 9781539035367

www.ingramcontent.com/pod-product-compliance
Lightning Source LLC
Chambersburg PA
CBHW060410190526
45169CB00002B/842